HWAET!

20 YEARS OF
LEDBURY POETRY
FESTIVAL

Mark Fisher was Labour MP for Stoke-on-Trent Central from 1983 to 2010, becoming opposition spokesman on arts and media following the 1987 general election, and later Minister for the Arts in 1997-98 before his sacking by Tony Blair. In 1992 he introduced his Right to Know private member's bill, the forerunner of the Freedom of Information Bill. He read English Literature at Cambridge, and before entering politics worked as a film producer and screenwriter, and from 1975 was principal of the Tattenhall Centre of Education in Cheshire, where Adrian Henri was Arts Council Poet in Residence (1979-81), succeeded by Liz Lochhead (1980-83)

One of his first engagements as Arts Minister was to open the first Ledbury Poetry Festival in 1997, and he has maintained his support for the festival as an active Patron over many years, and latterly also as editor of this anthology. His other publications include *Whose Cities* (with Ursula Owen, Penguin Books, 1991), *A New London* (with Richard Rogers, Penguin Books, 1992) and *Britain's Best Museums and Galleries* (Allen Lane, 2004). He lives in London.

COVER PHOTOGRAPHS: The cover shows poets reading at Ledbury Poetry Festival over the past 20 years. Clockwise, from left: Yang Lian, †Ko Un, Paul Muldoon, John Agard, †Michael Longley, Carol Ann Duffy, Jean 'Binta' Breeze, †Naomi Shihab Nye, †Antonella Anedda, Sara-Jane Arbury, †Patience Agbabi, Adrian Mitchell, Jack Mapanje, Kazuko Hohki (© Harry Rook 2013), Ian McMillan, †Emily Berry, Fleur Adcock, †Benjamin Zephaniah. Photos either commissioned by Ledbury Poetry Festival or taken by †Neil Astley.

HWAET!

20 YEARS OF LEDBURY POETRY FESTIVAL

edited by
MARK FISHER

ISBN: 978 1 78037 313 3

First published 2016 by
Bloodaxe Books Ltd,
Eastburn,
South Park,
Hexham,
Northumberland NE46 1BS
in association with
Ledbury Poetry Festival,
The Master's House,
Ledbury,
Herefordshire HR8 1EA.

www.bloodaxebooks.com   www.poetry-festival.co.uk
For further information about Bloodaxe or Ledbury
please visit our websites or write to the above addresses
for a catalogue or festival programme.

Supported using public funding by
**ARTS COUNCIL
ENGLAND**

ACKNOWLEDGEMENT

Proceeds from the sales of this book will assist Ledbury Poetry
Festival's educational work with schools and others. Many thanks
are due to an anonymous donor for kindly supporting this initiative.

Cover design: Neil Astley & Pamela Robertson-Pearce.

Printed in Great Britain by Bell & Bain Limited, Glasgow, Scotland, on
acid-free paper sourced from mills with FSC chain of custody certification.

CONTENTS

THE PEOPLE

Ledbury Poetry Festival

Ledbury Poetry Festival came about because a group of poetry enthusiasts living in the town twenty years ago made it happen, and it has been able to flourish since then because of the support it has received over two decades from many more dedicated people, as trustees, patrons, volunteers or staff, and with much needed financial assistance from Arts Council England and regular sponsors including in particular the Pennington-Mellor-Munthe Charity Trust and The Elmley Foundation.

The five founding trustees were Peter Arscott, John Burns, Margaret Rigby, Martyn Moxley and Richard Surman, with initial management by Blanca Rey Surman.

Charles Bennett was the first director to manage the creative programming in 2000. He was succeeded by the current artistic director, Chloe Garner, in 2006. Victoria Patch was the first festival manager in 2011, and was succeeded in 2015 by Phillippa Slinger. Sandra Dudley has been finance manager since 2010.

Key patrons have included Adam Munthe, benefactor and host of festival events at Hellens; Mark Fisher, who opened the first Ledbury Poetry Festival in 1997 as Labour arts minister; Ursula Owen and Juliet Stevenson.

The trustees are indebted also to numerous others who have helped the festival over the years, including all the visiting writers and performers, and most especially the people of Ledbury, who have not only wanted to come to the events but have helped as volunteers, accommodated poets in their homes and given over space in their shops and businesses to promote the festival.

ADAM MUNTHE

A Foreword

> Perhaps man really dies when his brain stops, when he loses
> the capacity to take in a new idea.
>
> GEORGE ORWELL

> The writer's task is to reshape an accurate and honest language
> that will permit communication…
>
> THOMAS MERTON

> Linguistic degeneration is both the product and the generator
> of economic and political decadence.
>
> ROWAN WILLIAMS

So what's poetry *for* again? Bath time with that echo from the water? For football matches, crude, rude, and noisy? For rap music and night clubs? For when you're in the middle of nowhere, without mobile phone, and to remind yourself that you're still there, that your voice is as strong as the wind, that you're not alone? Or for a moment of space, stillness, when you recall someone's clear voice whispering… and the magic of that whisper is concentrated into something close to perfection, and speaks to you, echoes in you, and in no one else! And also maybe because a rhyme is like music, and a rhythm gives you beat, pulse, the steps to somewhere else…?

So maybe poetry is for all these things… but first, what's poetry made of? Sounds…language…words of course…but pulled, shaped, stretched, twisted, tortured, rearranged to maximise a thought, a feeling, a sense, a disturbance, from just *one* brain and heart; from just one person's thinking, one man or woman's passion…through to you, me, personally and directly.

And if it's us – amateurs or professionals – doing the words, looking for the magic, attempting to write a piece of poetry, to encapsulate a thought, a moment, a joy – it's the same, and the first principle, the first engagement has to be with ourselves. And this business of finding a voice is crucial – it's what differentiates us from every other voice, and equally (no, more importantly) from the gang's, the group's, the mindless faceless fashionable herd's voice!

And how do we develop this skill to be ourselves, to characterise our own voices, not just as poets but as mindful, independent human beings? I submit that firstly we must require and develop in ourselves a capacity to distinguish honesty, clarity, from subterfuge and obfuscation.

Let's look at some examples: Language that is designed to be no one's in particular, the language of bureaucracy, manifesto, mission, regulation, the language of much of public life, of commercial interests, tax evasion, human rights violation, dictatorship, terrorism ...is the language of those whose interest is in avoiding communication and in avoiding argument. 'That is a language that sets out to conceal and ignore... a language that wants to shrink the world... *to what can be dealt with in the speaker's terms alone*' (Rowan Williams).

The practice of open exchange, confronting assumptions, "civil" (not to mention polite) disagreement – in other words good thinking ...speaking, writing – is meant to make the *other* pause and rethink; it insists that the world is larger than the 'other' thought... and is directed towards making a person see, and feel, and know *more*, not less! If we talk (and write) dishonestly, unanswerably, what we are doing is preparing for "confrontation" in its more terrible fancy dress; we are in effect preparing to reduce the 'other', for the annihilation of complexity and difference, for the elimination of humanity – ours *and* the other's... and finally we are making it easy for the enemy! George Orwell puts it like this: the choice for mankind is between freedom and happiness, and for the great bulk of mankind happiness is better.

Finally *all* that defends us from absolute power, which is absolute stasis, are words...used with integrity. Their importance is incalculable. Our responsibility, consequently, to future generations must be to provide our children with the means, and freedom, to use language to grow their perspectives, their thoughts, and feelings, to the outer limits of their capacites.

Poets, more than philosophers, logicians, politicians and preachers, teach us to break out of our own barriers of conditioning, and conformity. Yes, they teach us to think outside the box, certainly; they also show us how to think for *ourselves*, to think with an individual voice, to concentrate our language, passion, intelligence, into the most powerful space possible, where the extraneous is abandoned, and where words become music, being, remembrance ...and truer than true!

Last year our Ledbury Poetry Festival poets reached close to 3000 children in local schools in the West Midlands. We know from the Ofsted reports that vocabulary, articulation, and language skills are significantly improved where such an impetus is given. Words work of course! And real poets are essential to the process. They search and find the lies, and overturn their tricks; they paint images out of air, bring their truths to daylight with infinitely personal voices, add lilt to language with rhythm, rhyme, and a creative power which aims at the heart and soul of experience; and to a place where liberty is…and happiness! When poets teach us, and our children such freedoms, we can only offer gratitude.

Is there *anything* more important?

The limits of my language means the limits of my world.

LUDWIG WITTGENSTEIN

(With gratitude to Rowan Williams!)

MARK FISHER

Introduction: *Hwaet!*

Over the past 20 years more than 550 poets have read at Ledbury, including poets from more than 35 countries.

This anthology attempts to bring together a representative selection of those poets, together with the memories, stories and comments of some of them.

The festival has always nurtured new and young writers, and worked extensively with schools. Last year we worked with nearly 3000 children. The poets who took part in this had a dramatic effect on children's confidence, literacy and, of course, their writing ability: an effect noted by the Ofsted Inspectorate. The publication of this anthology will raise more funds to support the festival's important educational work, and we would like to thank the poets who have helped us by contributing their work, as well as the anonymous sponsor who has kindly offered to cover the book's costs.

This anthology demonstrates that, led by director Chloe Garner and patrons including Carol Ann Duffy and Ursula Owen, we are actively promoting the excellent work of women's poetry: in 2015 we staged a major poetry event, in Ledbury and in London, entitled *Dangerous Women*, and this anthology contains poems by 90 women, just under half the number of poets included.

Ledbury has an excellent record in welcoming poets from diverse backgrounds and from overseas, most recently Ko Un in 2015 and Mark Doty in 2016. At a time when depressingly few foreign novels or collections of poetry are published in Britain the 67 overseas poets included in this anthology give a glimpse of what we are missing.

We have much to celebrate. We are living in what may come to be seen as a Golden Age for poetry. The quality of the collections winning the T.S. Eliot and Forward Prizes in recent years, and the excellent work that publishers such as Bloodaxe, Carcanet, Faber and others are doing, suggests as much. As does that of Arc, who have given invaluable help in bringing together the work of overseas poets, and many other smaller presses whose poets have been given a platform at Ledbury.

The state of poetry in Britain, and in the wider world, is very much better than twenty years ago. We are determined that the next twenty years will show even more exciting developments.

An anthology like this is a collective effort. It would not have been possible without the contributions of Brenda Read-Brown, the Gloucestershire poet, who has tirelessly written to the contributors, chased them up and collated their offerings; and of Neil Astley, the founding editor of Bloodaxe and another Trustee of the Festival. Not only did he conjure the title, *Hwaet!* (always a problem with any book), but, more crucially, his incomparable knowledge of contemporary poetry (as demonstrated by Bloodaxe's *Staying Alive* trilogy), underpins this collection.

But at the centre of this anthology and of the festival itself is Ledbury's superb director, Chloe Garner. She has turned what was a good poetry festival into one that is (with all respect due to Aldeburgh, StAnza and others), the best in the country. She has had excellent support both from the festival trustees and fellow staff (Victoria Patch, manager until last year, and now Phillippa Slinger, along with Sandra Dudley), but it is Chloe's determination and vision that have transformed the Festival.

So let us celebrate the first twenty years of this wonderful festival, and look forward to the coming decades.

CHLOE GARNER

A Festival of Generosity

One volunteer, Fran Bradley, launched the Poets in Schools' programme 20 years ago and we are still partners in this wonderful enterprise today. Generosity!

Poets travel from all over the world to offer their poetry to our audiences and support the festival through their blogs and their enthusiastic online "likes". Generosity!

Our community of volunteers work in the office, open up their homes, give people lifts (sometimes long distances for trains and planes), steward and manage events. Make poetic fairy trails, dream catchers and cushions, graffiti the streets with poetry. Generosity!

Those of you who buy lots of tickets, listen intently, ask questions, buy books. Generosity!

Those of you who risk events with poets and performers you have never heard of. Or in weird and wonderful locations – underwater at Ledbury Swimming Pool, surrounded by the 400-year-old frescoes in Kempley Church, at an all-nighter at Hellens Manor. That is generosity and I thank you for it!

I spent my first few years at every festival on edge, in case something went wrong. Things do go wrong, but they are often sorted by the time I arrive. Generosity!

So I have learned to try to relax a little. What good fortune to meet poetic heroes including Sharon Olds, Tony Harrison and John Burnside. To discover many wonderful poets including Naomi Shihab Nye, Jane Hirshfield, Valérie Rouzeau, Marcelijus Martinaitis, Amjad Nasser, Paula Meehan, Martín Espada, C.D. Wright, Eavan Boland – I could go on and on.

In my experience, people come to the festival with an openhearted and open-minded aittude. Curious and willing to make new discoveries, meet new people, experience chance-happenings. I think we all cherish these memories of unexpected and wonderful encounters. The Estonian poet, Kristiina Ehin and her fellow musicians bursting into song as they stroll down Church Lane; relaxing in the sunshine outside Shedman's shed with Idler Tom Hodgkinson; lunch in the presence of three formidable women,

Clare Short, Ursula Owen and Juliet Stevenson. It is out of this spirit – of willing open-heartedness – that the special atmosphere of each festival is born.

Over the course of ten days the events start to feel like a conversation. Poets attend one other's readings and when they give their own performance they respond to what they have heard. Generosity!

The festival takes on a momentum of connection and themes can emerge completely by chance. The intensity of the experience builds and I am like a cup brimming – my head is ringing with poetry. It is inspiring. Then by the last day or two I must discreetly wipe away tears. I like to think this is not just because I am tired! It is because I have immersed myself in poetry for ten days and am hyper-sensitised. Freshly receptive to what I hear.

Poetry holds magic. It touches on mysteries that I can't articulate but that move me deeply. It certainly challenges and stimulates me. All art is an act of generosity, as much as it is a necessity for the artist and I am grateful to have benefited so completely from this. I know people who come to the festival feel the same and I see it in their eyes when they come to me to say thank you. So I would like to say, on behalf of us all, *thank you poets!*

I love Ledbury and even more during the festival. The town has a special and distinctly poetic eccentricity and colour. Poetry is embraced here, poetry matters, people care, the town is engaged with this joyous celebration of words, poems and poets. This is remarkable. This is generosity!

PETER ARSCOTT

In this digital and virtual age, an expression of culture is a simple way to truly connect with others and bring down barriers. It is also a defence against standardisation, and an opportunity to build a sense of community and place that allows people a special experience, and fulfils a growing demand for the many rewards that come from listening to poetry or music with your fellow human beings, or from watching a film entirely written in verse or from tramping the Malvern Hills at night as part of a writers' extreme workshop, or from simply being at a festival.

It's good for the soul.

Art means nothing without people, and the Ledbury Poetry Festival has for the last two decades been a stimulating, engaging, questioning and challenging experience in our cultural calendar thanks to the many like-minded staff and volunteers, trustees and chairs, poets and performers, patrons, funders and visitors who make it happen every year. This festival owes them everything.

JOHN BURNS

Of the Ledbury friends and neighbours who first got together in December 1995, I doubt if between us we knew the names of more than a dozen living and published poets. But we did know how to put on a party and that proved to be the key: the poets and the poetry seemed to follow of themselves.

The festival was always an ensemble production, where the success of any particular event could owe as much to the warmth of the stewards' smiles as to the brilliance of the performer or the genius of the directors' scheduling. We were a notoriously fractious team, some of us barely on speakers by July 1997, but the clashing temperaments seemed to balance each other creatively, and however tetchy the quarrelling, nobody ever put their egos before the goals of the festival.

Advice for my successors? Never try living for ten days on black coffee, tonic water, Marlboros and nerves; though I'm glad I did once.

MARTYN MOXLEY

The pitfalls and pleasures of a passion for poetry. The plagiarist threatened with imprisonment... and a mention by Thunderer in *The Times* for hanging on to a risque Chaucer script. The peeping-tom... an attempt to quieten distracting noise from an adjacent garden turning into a heated exchange with an irate husband. The phantom scene stealer... getting caught by Benjamin Zephaniah trying to lurk anonymously back stage twiddling the sound system. The pleasantest of peregrinations with poets in residence...the view from Hay bluff with Naomi Shihab Nye...to Hereford with Billy Collins...and Gillian Clarke...and Carol Ann Duffy. The plumply festive pie of the cider supper and its gatherings of poets in peaceful potation. And those final group hugs of festivals fruitfully finished.

RICHARD SURMAN

The origins of the Ledbury Poetry Festival were modest and more than a little eccentric: of the original group that got together to discuss the idea of a poetry festival, a disparate "gang of six" emerged: a former blue badge guide turned artist, a joiner, a photographer, an organic farmer, a teacher and a former information officer with the British Tourist Association.

The original idea had been a series of gatherings of poets in local pubs, but the energy, experience and imagination of the "gang of six" gave it a super boost, even in the first year. With very little money, a lot of support from the local community, some energetic and intelligent fund-raising and brass necked cheek, our first festival included Sir Roy Strong, George Melly and a number of nationally known poets including John Cooper Clarke and John Hegley. It was an intoxicating mix of poetry, music and town involvement.

Vivid memories of those early days include "borrowing" a Steinway from Llandaff cathedral for the jazz pianist Stan Tracey and Mike Horovitz (and watching in horror as the stage in St Katherine's Hall sagged under its weight), our first town party with a local folk group in the pouring rain under the 17th-century

Market House, dragging Johnny Clarke off the stage when it looked as if he was going to go on for the whole night, upsetting the Ledbury in Bloomers with some ill-considered comments about foaming marigolds, stopping the memorial clock in St Katherine's Hall because it was putting a performer off his stroke, Carol Ann Duffy being heckled in St Michael's church – and then the whole thing exploded into the second year, with the whole town rocking to an eight-piece salsa band in the town centre one warm evening.

We all had different ideas as to what we wanted to achieve and how: for the most part we managed to combine our ideas harmoniously. My particular interest was in giving all the poets and performers the best possible technical support and for that we developed an excellent partnership with the Malvern Theatre technical team: not all poets read their work well or clearly!

There was intense pleasure in seeing this delightful and sleepy Herefordshire market town spring to life each summer, immense pleasure too in seeing young people from local schools wake up to the fact that poetry was an important part of life. When we started the Ledbury Poetry Festival in 1996, none of us had any sense that it would grow into one of the UK's major literary events, now celebrating its 20th anniversary.

PETER CARTER

One especially treasured festival memory would be C.K. Williams contemplating the Frost cottage at Leddington while leaning on a five-barred gate. We had to get back to Ledbury for his reading but it was with the greatest reluctance that he tore himself away from that spot. He had become rooted.

Another would be Michael Donaghy in our kitchen, accompanying Ruth Padel on his wooden flute.

Or the whole visit by Samuel Menashe, another greatly missed poet. This came about after Stephen Crook, librarian of the Berg Collection in the New York Public Library, met him at a reading in New York. Stephen was known to us through shared interest in John Masefield, and inferring from their conversation that Menashe would 'like to cross the pond again', wrote accordingly to our mutual friend Linda Hart, knowing of her connection to Ledbury Poetry Festival. Linda in turn passed the word on to me, and by happy chance it just so happened that Diana and I had met Menashe at Hay in 1997. We'd talked, as one does, and he gave us a photocopy of his poem 'Eyes'. Not one to underplay his hand, Samuel suggested that we look out for the Penguin Modern Poets volume he shared with Donald Davie and Allen Curnow.

Chloe Garner picked up the baton and thus Samuel Menashe, with help from the National Endowment for the Arts, came to Ledbury in 2008. He had time for everyone and charmed all whom he met. He entertained his rapt audiences at two events, a Poet to Poet event with Maurice Riordan, and an interview and reading with Christopher Ricks. He was the perfect house guest. The only cloud concerned a close friend in hospital in New York. Samuel asked whether he might use our phone to call his friend which he did, daily. After two or three such calls he announced, with his usual charm, that he would not insult our hospitality by offering to pay.

ALAN LLOYD

The sheer exhilaration of booking our first poet (Wendy Cope) and names to conjure with: Carol Ann Duffy, Matthew Sweeney, Liz Lochhead, Dannie Abse, Michael Donaghy, Robin Robertson, John Hegley, plus George Melly to open the first festival, give a vulgar after-dinner speech and consume a bottle of Jameson's. Melly opened an exhibition by his friend, Conroy Maddox, last of the English surrealists, who, amazingly, was born in Ledbury. Peter Barkworth was merciless with the amateurs in our Reading Allowed event. Simon Armitage was late and we tried not to panic, while we crammed the Feathers' old ballroom, and then some more, for John Cooper Clarke, who was reluctant to go on and the likes of whom Ledbury had not seen before.

Germaine Greer said she would leave immediately after *Desert Island Poems* and stayed late into the night, talking and drinking. We hosted *Any Questions* simultaneously, and both events sold out.

Carol Ann was heckled in the church: *The World's Wife* was

deemed blasphemous, even though the rector in the front row didn't mind one bit.

We lost the band during the interval at a town party. John Walsh lost his children.

We got into deep trouble stopping the clock in St Katherine's Hall but Adrian Mitchell refused to perform unless we did – so we did, and it made headline news nationally and we learnt rapidly how to get publicity.

An audience member fainted heavily during an Elizabeth Barrett Browning event at Hope End performed by Penelope Leach, Roy Strong and Peggy Reynolds. And yes, there was a doctor in the house, well a surgeon.

Prunella Scales and Jeremy Paxman were (separately) very nervous before going on.

John Hegley wanted to visit Kilpeck church.

Some performers attracted swathes of groupies (U.A. Fanthorpe), while some brought their parents (Michael Moloney).

You need stamina as an organiser, especially if there are Celtic poets in the offing, who can carouse until the wee hours. But after-hours performances could be memorable: Jack Mapanje and Yang Lian crooning in dialects learnt at their mothers' knees, while the macho players in the salsa band didn't know where to look as an innocent-looking Clare Pollard recited rude poems.

It was fun.

THE POETS

ROBERT ADAMSON   ■ AUSTRALIA

The Long Bay Debating Society

I spent my twenty-first in Long Bay Penitentiary
Each day in the front yards
We paced up and down
At night I read novels
And the poetry of Percy Shelley
Sometimes an education officer
Would turn up and ask
What are you going to do with your future?
I'd tell him I wanted to be a poet
He would shake his head
And comment I was being insolent
After weeks I convinced him
We wanted to start a debating team
There were plenty of crims
Who would join up
It took a month to convince the Governor
Finally the authorities agreed
We could form debating society
Things went well and we attended library
And researched our topics
Then came the day a team
From the outer agreed to come inside
And conduct a debate with us
However there was a condition
The Governor would chose the topic
Eventually the prison librarian
Ceremoniously handed us the Governor's note
(it was the summer of 1964) our topic
'Is the Sydney Opera House Really Necessary?'

The sleeping-bag

But when we rolled him out he didn't move:
curled up like a bud. He'd fallen asleep
snuggled in the back of the Land Rover,

and Barry thought it would be amusing
to tote him up all those endless steps
to wherever we were visiting

like a sack of coal, over his shoulders,
swaddled in impermeable down.
Just hooliganism, really; a joke.

It may have taken seconds, not long minutes,
to shake him and shake him...
                              Light of my life
(child of my first marriage – nothing to Barry).

I have some friends who lost a son that way,
smothered in an airless den of feathers;
which, if I'd known... But not my son, praise God.

Barry could get away with most things.
Kids thought he was magic. They came flocking.
He was to kill five boys in his time:

by negligence, by booze, by his grievous fault.
They drowned, all five of them together, trapped
in a vehicle, unsupervised.

But my boy wasn't one of them.
(Let me not gloat, Lord. Let me not gloat.)
We'd moved on by then, I and my boy.

JOHN AGARD

The Jester's Eureka Moment

How do you fuse
a Muslim and a Jew into one?
is a question the jester
would many a day brood on
as he squatted on his futon.

At last – a win-win solution.
Since flesh dwelleth in the Word,
I'll start by changing my name
to Abdul Abdullah Goldberg,
or simply Suleyman Solomon

and under my yarmulke dome
to holy Mecca I shall roam
seeking kaaba in kabbalah
as I do my salaam shalom
from dusk onto dawn.

May the mind's credos be exiled
from the orchard of my heart.
And may Yahweh and Allah smile
as I whirl down the aisle
with my chosen gentile.

And when reckoning day comes
and this jester bursts into atoms
for being one of God's scapegoats,
may yours truly be timely bombed,
not by one side, but by both.

And from folly's ever-blossoming bed,
let wisdom regather itself bud by bud.
Of course, easier said than done,
when dogma wags the mind by the tail
and heart forgets the scent of the frail.

PATIENCE AGBABI

Museum (1590)
(FROM Chains)

From dawn to dusk and dusk to dawn, I, slave
to Sir John Hawkins, bound, emblackened crest
upon his coat of arms of lion and wave,
salute him, founder of the Chatham Chest
that succours seamen maimed in the Armada;
salute him true in Spanish, French, Italian;
salute him, most courageous founding father
of Chatham Dockyard and the 'race built gallion':
But race, my race, is how you built your wealth
O founder of the English trade in flesh
and yet in selling me, you sell yourself –
in this heraldic sign, our fates enmesh.
I, the proud crest in history's glass case:
What see you when you look upon my face?

This poem is from a corona of sonnets written while Patience Agbabi was Poet-in-Residence at the Historic Dockyard at Chatham, Kent, where each sonnet was displayed outside the various sites named in their titles.

FADHIL AL-AZZAWI   ■ IRAQ

Unsuccessful Film

In the movie house of my bleeding soul,
lying back on my dream couch,
I see myself in a film
running daily for eternity.

It is snowing. This is St Petersburg, glorious in its rags
singing alone in the dark.
Carriages with sleepy horses trot past leisurely,
and along the sidewalks
drunks are hunting prostitutes.

I am in a tavern, on the table a bottle of vodka.
From my corner I see Raskolnikov, a German cap on his head,
wrapped in his tattered overcoat,
shuffling along, followed by his greedy widow,
to pledge to me his bloody hatchet.

Near a bus stop in a public square crowded with tourists
Hamlet appears suddenly. He grabs my hand:
'Prithee, poet, write my story anew,
I am a man, take me for all I am
and let me be happy again.'

Opening his heart, confessing his foolish scruples
croaking in his head like a crow
in his castle in Denmark:
'I am thy father's spirit;
doom'd for a certain term to walk the night.'
He asks me to free him from his father's ghost.

On the gateway of forgotten Ur-zaqura
I hear the cry of Enkido, carried by the dead
in a boat crossing seas of firebrand and burning water
on their way to the underworld.
I see Gilgamesh emerge out of a crack
in the wall of my cold house
like a friend, lost for centuries, now coming back:
'Let us go together! Be my guide!'
So we go deep into the forest
looking for the deceiver serpent
that stole his magic plant.

Figures in tales and epics, told to the children.
Figures of wars that had been won
and others lost.

Figures made of tin to be sold in the brass market.
Figures of straw (all they need is a matchstick).
Figures for decoration at festivals.
Figures to be remembered,
Figures to be forgotten.

Vagabonds, villains, philosophers and kings,
generals, wise men and poets,
all come to me as shadows,
escaped from their time-traps
to enter my heart.
They come one by one and knock at my door.
Confused, I open and welcome them in.

Oh, damn, how I did I find myself in this valley of the dead?
Who led these souls to my gloomy house?
Oh, this is not my story, Oh I am not God
to carry the sins of mankind on my shoulders.

But as it often happens,
I get up haunted with fear and wonder,
I grope blindly for the light switch
and see myself in the world again.

Outside in the street, I hear the trees
singing for me in the wind.

Thank God! I say to myself,
now I can sleep in peace
and forget this unsuccessful film.

translated from the Arabic by the author

MARAM AL-MASSRI

from Barefoot Souls

I have seen them.
Those women
with faces camouflaged in blue,
those women
with bruises hidden between their thighs,
their dreams captured, their words silenced,
those women
with their weary smiles.

I have seen them
all
pass by in the street,
barefoot souls
looking over their shoulders,
worried about being followed,
fearing the footsteps of some storm;
thieves of the moon, they pass
in the guise of ordinary women.
Nobody can recognise them
except for those
who are of their kind.

translated from the French by Theo Dorgan

BASEM AL-NABRISS

No cherries in Gaza

• On white hearts
red missiles
fell.

• In its makeshift grave
the newborn
dreams of milk.

• The skies quake
the snail persists
in its summer sleep.

• Female soldiers left
many dead bodies. A few condoms.

• The missile lands. The roach emerges
from the sewage.

• Rafah: August 3
four old women
eight drones.

• Twins were parted:
one half to an anonymous grave
another to an anonymous breast.

• A pitch-black night
From above the pilot detects everyone's location
From our houses we detect every star.

• Haiku in blood. No cherries in Gaza

• Mute sky.
On the balcony pupils dilate.

- In the wake of the *Merkavah*
only the nettle
keeps growing.

- On a straw mat
remnants of tomatoes
Death crosses generations.

- F-16 pilot. A post-modern monotheistic god.

- Evening approaches
A canary is dying
away from its owner.

- Under the delicate twilight
they buried whole bodies
and returned incomplete.

- The generous pilot
distributes his imported gifts
over the poor land.

- Escaping from East Rafah
I encountered en route
massacred palms.

- From the sky above the sea
after two launches
the pilot returns bored.

- And who are you?
I am the next round
Hereafter I'll visit you in nightmares,
oh my baby.

translated by Tal Nitzán

Merkavah (chariot), the name of an Israeli military tank. Translated from a Hebrew translation of the original Arabic poem. Thanks: Avi Elkayam, Mohammed Abd El-Dayem Hendam, Morani Kornberg-Weiss. [TN]

AL-SADDIQ AL-RADDI

Poem

I saw the angel
and the singing birds slaughtered.
I saw the horse,
the soldiers,
the grieving women,
the dead trees, and other women
inured to screams and wailing.
I saw the streets, the gusting wind,
the sports cars
racing by, the boats, the innocent kids.

I said, 'Master of the Water, this is
how things are: tell me about the clay,
the fire, the smoke, the shadows, the smell
of reality.' Deliberately, I did not ask
about our homes.

translated from the Arabic by Mark Ford & Hafiz Kheir

NICK ALEXANDER

A Heron

A heron
in a grey tail-coat
standing still and silent in the river's rushing shallows
zen-poised and arrow-beaked
ignored me on the
river path
until I
came
too
close and crossed
the invisible boundary line
of his wariness to disturb his
concentration, causing him to rise on
those coat-tail wings just for two or
three languid flaps. I stopped again
as he settled back down and I waited
to watch him fish. He did not move
a muscle and seemed content to
contemplate the fishiness of the
water, the water that should
be   sluicing through his
beak. We repeated our
ballet with each step I
took.   Eventually   I
swung out wider; he
rose into the air
to circle back
around. Then
he   resumed
his   former
posture. I,
I moved
on to
less
el
e
g
a
n
t
company.

AL ALVAREZ

Night Life

My dreams are getting worse. Lord, how I miss you.
We're sleeping side by side, but in my dreams
You're out of reach and dwindling,
And when you turn to wave your eyes are clouded
With all that grief. I have to look away.

In dreams the car won't start, the train has left without us
And the world is falling apart. Then suddenly
There you are again and here we are,
Hand in hand in the dark like babes in the wood.
'Please,' I say in my dream. 'Sorry,' you answer,
'Sorry, it can't be done.' And then I wake.

ANTONELLA ANEDDA   ■ ITALY

[Untitled]

> The sea is full of exiles, the rocks covered with blood
>   TACITUS: *Historiae*

I think today of those two, among the many drowned
a few yards from this sunny coast,
found under the hull tightly clasped together.
I wonder if coral can grow from their bones
and what will become of their blood in the salt,
so then I study – searching out among my father's
old books of forensic medicine a manual
where, undifferentiated, the victims and the criminals
are photographed: suicides, murderers, genital organs.

No landscapes, just the iron sky of the photos,
occasionally a chair, a body covered by a sheet, bare feet
on a camp bed. I read, and discover that the precise term
is livor mortis. Blood gathers below and clots
first red then livid purple till it turns to dust
and so yes it can disperse itself amid the salt.

translated from the Italian by Jamie McKendrick

SARA-JANE ARBURY

The next train to depart from platform 2 is the 10.40 Central Trains service to Hereford. Calling at...

Found moments. Glimpses. One minute there.
Next instant. Lost. A flock of waterbirds unfurling
paper white wings, following the horseshoe river
into dusk. Pollen caught in sunlight, whirling
in a flurry of faery after the train, slow
past Leominster station. Two horizons –
there! Spotted through rain on the bus window;
a trick of the clouds above the Malverns.
Another herd of Herefords, mapped with red,
earth made animal, their whitened faces
grounded in the county. Breath... look ahead,
catch sight of winter, the fingertraces
of sheep in snow, frosted ice on the Wye,
apple trees in white wedded to the sky.

This is the first poem in *County Lines*, a series of nine sonnets inspired by Sara-Jane Arbury's encounters as Writer-in-Residence for Herefordshire in 2005-07. *County Lines* was premièred at Ledbury Poetry Festival in 2007.

SIMON ARMITAGE

The Subconscious

Arrives with his daughter, she's all braced teeth
and blunderbuss freckles, she bolts
from the passenger seat
of his Fiat Doblo and gallops
with two dogs into the garden. It's Sunday.
Now suddenly here in his hand

the awkward contraption:
steel forks either end of a steel collar,
galvanised spring and trigger,
toothed prongs that snap down –
he throws back his head – it's instant.
The girl and dogs play chase

near the sundial. The lawn's a bombsite –
he strides along curved archipelagos
of heaped soil, probes the turf
with a wooden dabble,
with a silver trowel intrudes
into dark tunnels – see,

the walls are rounded and fossil-smooth
as if burrowed by serpents –
lowers four primed traps,
tamps down loose earth
then marks each site
with a metal rod flying a coloured ribbon.

He knows my sister.
One dog's a pet, the grey one's a ratter.
A week on Monday
he's back on his own,
it's snowed, scrapes away snow
with his instep, raises

three traps choked with dirt, in the fourth
something hangs in the jack-knifed pincers,
a soft cosh or limp rubber tube
or a stuffed sock – that's how it looks
from the bedroom window.
Tosses it into a hessian sack, the mini-flagpoles

slide into a quiver. The doorbell.
Takes off his gloves, offers his pink hand:
he does wasps, vermin, I wouldn't believe
the damage caused by a single roe deer.
When he's gone I pitchfork
frozen volcanoes into the tractor-trailer.

NIC AUBURY

Job description

The title 'poet' comprehends
A multitude of sins,
And redefines where 'freelance' ends
And 'unemployed' begins.

MONA ARSHI

Seashells

The children are collecting
     shells again.

     Their ankles steeped
in the sand against the tide's swell.

They bring me milky broken offerings
     and other whole

     glazed perfections;
a silvery rainbowed mouth and others

sucked to spectral echoes. But this one
     here, with a twisted spine

     is my daughter's favourite;
she's already begun to adopt its perforated

useless rooms. She places it in her pocket
     strumming it with her thumb.

SHAKILA AZIZZADA   ■ AFGHANISTAN

Kabul

If my heart beats
for Kabul,
it's for the slopes of Bala Hissar,
holding my dead
in its foothills.

Though not one, not one
of those wretched hearts
ever beat for me.

If my heart grieves
for Kabul,
it's for Leyla's sighs of
'Oh, dear God!'
and my grandmother's heart
set pounding.

It's for Golnar's eyes
scanning the paths
from dawn to dusk, spring to autumn,
staring so long
that all the roads fall apart
and in my teenage nightmares
side roads
suddenly shed their skins.

If my heart trembles
for Kabul,
it's for the slow step of summer noons,
siestas in my father's house which,
heavy with midday sleep,
still weighs on my ribs.
For the playful Angel of the Right Shoulder
who keeps forgetting
to ward away stray bullets.

It's for the hawker's cry
of the vegetable seller doing his rounds,
lost in my neighbours' troubled dreams,
that my heart's trembling.

translated from the Dari by Mimi Khalvati & Zuzanna Olszewska

Bala Hissar: an ancient citadel in Kabul with a cemetery outside its walls.
Angel of the Right Shoulder: one of the angelic *Keraman Katebin*, who sit on
the shoulders of believers, recording their good and evil deeds.

The Song of the Husband

(for Johnny van der Westhuizen)

At 8am on Tuesdays and Thursdays in a class
on *Troilus and Criseyde* at the University of Cape Town,
taught by the only Black scholar in the Department of English,
I thought I learned of deathless love and its forgetting.

But years later in the line at the post office, he said
I should have left years ago,
there was so little time
before my wife died
what is there now

I knew it was to us he had given
those years and some sense of belonging
because he looked like us
and wielded Oxford behind his name,
like the armour we all needed.

What did I learn of love in that class,
not after all that our fragile choices are eternal
nor that the fateful gift,
the brooch or handkerchief,
is the thing that betrays us.

But that the sacrifice lies elsewhere,
in our most faithful acts, of staying,
of choosing good over love,
us over her.

Today, on the news of his death, I remember
the end always comes too early
the end comes too early
yet love is there, and deathless

JO BELL

SBJ

pip pip
pip pip
A bulb of bird inside the hedge, and seagulls
cutting round the bay. The day is lit with singing
from the nameless fellow in the bush.

We *call* it song. For all we know it might be
nightclub banter, liturgy or shouting;
no sense of anything but urgency as bird-buds bloom
under the likelihood of brighter days, and call.

And here's the little gorse chap – head back in thorns,
his slight flank pinking in the ready light
between the needles, tail a bellows
pumping out the notes:
pip pip
pip pip

No twitcher, me. A bird's a bird. I don't know
the word we use to understand him by
but nor, of course, does he; whose only calling
is to sing. And summer's in his eye.

SBJ: 'small brown job', the ornithologist's slang for an unidentifiable dull bird.

CHARLES BENNETT

New Come Over

On the map it looks like a ruled line of water
running from Lord's Holt to Moreton's Leam,

but once you find yourself at New Come Over
on a day in early spring when unruly gusts

have grabbed your map and made a bedraggled bird
from its narrow folds, you'll see how a banner of sky

has been laid on the ground, like a runway for clouds
polished with the rush of take-off –

a playground slide for your eye to be guided away
and out along a scroll of indelible blue

which now and forever is superimposing itself
on whatever you see, so that as you follow

the wake of two swans who paddle through air
you're falling deeper and further into the uplift.

EMILY BERRY

Drunken Bellarmine
(after Renee So)

In this spirit of affliction I beheld two things,
that shame is also revelry, and a body
is a spillage, or an addiction. I do not know
if this thing belongs to me, tipped-up set of weights

that promises, but never delivers, equilibrium.
I cannot make manifest this collection of feelings,
but look at me: I want to be loved for the wrong reasons.
I mean I want to be hated for the right reasons.
I have been lonely. Every time I say the word 'I'
I am ashamed. When I say 'I want' I am triply
ashamed. I want my shame to be a kind of proof
that deduces the world, and that's the worst
shame of all. I have been theatrical, entropic,
parting with myself for company. This heartsore
will not stop weeping and look, the sky is sick,
knitted too tightly; my face is up your sleeve
like a card trick. *DON'T LOVE ME:* I am guilty,
fatalistic and sticky round the mouth like a dirty baby.
I am a shitting, leaking, bloody clump of cells,
raw, murky and fluorescent, you couldn't take it.

LIZ BERRY

Connemara

I stepped out of my skin
that dusk in Connemara
where bush crickets thrummed
like pylons
and the lane smelled
of tar and clover.
What lay beneath
was fragile, not yet
ready for its season.
The drizzle
made sore music
of my nerve endings.
I was beautiful to the crows
as a butcher's window.

In the dusk, I was glorious,
so raw I felt each mote.
Kites beheld
my glowing jellyfish brain.
My heart was carmine,
radiant as a saint
in a wayside shrine.
I raised my arms
to the sky
and the air kissed me
with its stinging
worshipful mouth.

I threw the skin to the wind,
that sweet sack
I had tended and punished
for thirty-three years.
Now moths would make
heaven of it.
Let them come,
I thought,
I am ready;
for inside me you pulsed,
single-celled,
extraordinary.

SUJATA BHATT

A Neutral Country

He just wanted to step out
for a walk – some fresh air
to clear his head – and on the way back
he told his wife, he'd get some milk and eggs.
But he found dead bodies in front of his door,
five dead bodies, all young, all so young,
he repeats. It will take him a long time
to recover from this.
Now he prefers to stay at home.

*

One day a letter arrives,
an invitation, we accept –
We agree to visit a neutral country.

We cross rivers and valleys and mountains.
It is a quiet journey.
A strange brightness surrounds us.

*

Over here the air smells of cheese.
The first light in the morning
comes through layers of fog.

White gauze – endless veils –

And somewhere along the paths
we cannot see, somewhere, they tell us
Psyche walks, Eurydice walks –

They want us to believe –

We know there are cows somewhere
                    and church bells
waiting to be heard – But now
even the grapes are asleep.

*

They let us stay in one of their castles
and ask us to entertain their King.

Their King arrives with apples and honey,
                    with chocolate and coffee.
Their King arrives with a violin
                    and bottles of wine.

We never know what to say to him
and listen to his stories instead.

*

It's a castle protected by roses,
a castle protected by a lake.

Their lake smells of the dreams of birds –
there are dreams they call ghosts
and dreams they call fish.

Somehow they know what birds believe.

Their fish are alive and smell of nothing.
The lake's water smells of winter –
as if winter breathes within it.

The lake's water holds the memory
of a silver necklace once forgotten in the grass –

*

Afternoons we sit in their rose garden
and watch bees follow the sun.

Their roses are so fragrant
our hearts ache – our hearts ache
and we do not know why.

We watch lizards turn into leaves
and leaves turn into lizards.
We listen to the soft scraping, rustling sound
of their flight as they race down
the steps of the castle.
Even the oldest, most beautiful stones
cannot keep them.

But a nun follows the lizards
to a graveyard – and there she sings
to them until they dance.
She shows us how she does this
day after day – and we watch the way she turns
towards the roses.

*

It is August, early August –
before sundown –
        and as we walk through
            their vineyards
we can feel shadows turn gold.

*

We have forgotten to count the days,
forgotten why we came here.

They ask us to look at the stars,
at the moon – they ask us to believe –

RUTH BIDGOOD

Enigma

I've never been sure that, when the brain
drops into death, it takes with it
all that jumble of half-remembered
sights and sounds, half-shaped ideas, hauntings,
atmospheres, premonitions – the hinterland
of a departing life.
                              More likely, I've thought,
that gallimaufry escapes dark sleep, floats free,
its diverse entities gone sliding – can it be
randomly? – through chinks and windings
into a living brain, bringing bafflement, or even
once in a while unlooked-for hope of meaning.

Whence does that quirk of roadway come
I've visualised so often, twisting up
past a pale field of unfamiliar corn
and damply mirroring a darkening sky?
This picture has no feeling of memory, seems
to have no part in any life of mine.

Yet it has forced an enigmatic,
determined way into this brain that works
and works at it, finding no answers,
only a sense of what may be mine
by adoption – a possible meaning
endlessly to be sought, for a richness
hidden within it, wanted, apprehended,
not yet understood.

JULIA BIRD

The Preservation of Flowers

Between the cab firm and the chicken shop
the pavement cracked and a flower stall sprang up,
the city's special offer to the passer by.
It stocks every colour flower except grey,
twenty-four seven blossom, the odds on bees,
and a sign which says *You Can Smell The Flowers for Free*.
It checks the street. Those who used to hurry
are slowed, and sold on bouquets of *gorgeous* and *sorry*.
They pick the florist too. He's a bunch
of bluebell eyes and blooming sales pitch,
daisy grin and hip-slung money belt,
lily pollen brushed across his shirt.
Certain customers, he slips an extra rose
in the dozen; to certain customers he says
'Angel – if you want them to last a little bit longer
add a teaspoon of sugar to the water.'

■ Congratulations on your 20th birthday, Ledbury! I've been a reader, a listener and a co-producer with you over the years, and never had anything other than a stimulating, social and wonderful time. [JB]

EAVAN BOLAND

Local History

The century darkens. The small cities of a continent,
the customs they stored, the waterways

which opened out for commerce and leave-taking
are still there waiting
in the near-sighted dusks of a coastal winter.

But this is our neighbourhood, our consolation.

The roads go from here to the rivers.
The rivers run back down in the rain.

I see you passer-by as you drive down
our street. I imagine how
I rush away in your rear-view mirror.
                                        Trust this
to be local history. Or at least a version of it.

SEAN BORODALE

Otters

Like something this river was supposed to be hiding
was disturbed.

Thickness of air, the water like gravel;
turning corner of an eye.

The gloomy mist
and the green gloom particular early morning

rain, pending storm, the dragged sky's ruin;
everything just conscious –

until a dull thud, a scuffle, insistence of water
tearing along the lowest trail of the valley; the river-
wet:

face of some kind, thick roots moving
under the hot weird smell of nettles;

the air telepathic between brain and plant;
the river corridor wild with alder;

a tensed cloth-weave of milliseconds, a hissing
after-puncture, a versatile there:

otter, and otter.

One near, the other downstream
dips, lengthens, and bends its tailing.

I in the flicker,
the distilled, whole spectrum of otter
breathing above meniscus:
portraying me hearing it.

The whole river
jinked along its axis.

Run to the house,
I caught this shy part of the river, out there.
The kitchen voices: *can we see?*
Boots. Rush.
But they've gone: water trembling along an edge.

Search the ruffled normality
for nothing.
Did they see? Did they see?

River ripped, dipping iron eyes into flowing dark.
Eyes that could absorb
towards light, or exit.

ALISON BRACKENBURY

Ninety-seven

He had that art, too, counting sheep,
my grandfather, away at ten
at shows. Surprising he could read,
and he could count. I spent all day
high on his hills, watched clouds lift fair
over the lambing hut's bent chimney.
Is there a photo? Who would care?

My grandfather cared for the sheep,
before lunch tins, pulled pipe from mouth
to count them as they crammed three deep,
'Thirteen, fourteen,' never missing
his beat, as fleeces pressed trough's edge.
'Ninety-seven. Eh. Three missing.'
He hauled three, struggling, from a hedge.

The shepherd died. The sheep are gone.
Some, of course, slid onto plates.
Rams were exported, blood count wrong.
When the last collie was put down
the Ministry bought the flock for tests.
How lives must shrink, although along
the hill, clouds sweep, the tin hut rusts.

Out of dark spring, the swifts flash back.
I watch them from a valley town.
Their crying drowns the church's clock.
They ride air like a surfer down
his wave. Their blue is blank with heat.
I scarcely know where I have been
but plant my feet on fresh ground, count
not sheep but swifts. 'Thirteen, fourteen –'

■ The last verse of 'Ninety-seven' is set in Ledbury, in 2013, during one of the sunniest festival weekends.

I have many memories of Ledbury Poetry Festival, some flooded by sunlight, some by water. But my favourite is a brief meeting in 2015 with the Festival Director, Chloe Garner.

Chloe wasn't leaving an executive committee, or poring over a laptop. She was carrying a brimming bucket of water down the plunging stairs from the Hospitality Room, ready for a children's poetry and craft event in a July garden.

On the way, she was intercepted by a kindly volunteer, who took charge of the bucket! I think both encounters show why Ledbury, in sun and rain, remains one of the friendliest and best-loved of Britain's many poetry festivals. [AB]

ALAN BROWNJOHN

Making a Difference

On an idle afternoon I sat in a park
that was clean and green and sunlit, and saw
a lady who liked children (she herself
having been a child once) call *Hullo, Hul*-lo
to three small-to-medium girls she recognised
because she was a relation, or neighbour, or friend
– like a less demanding mother than the one
in charge of them. She also said *Hullo!* to a boy
who pulled with him a red and green wooden horse
on bumping wheels, very rare these days…
Beside us were goldfish ponds, a clock of flowers
that faithfully struck the hour trembling all its petals,
and a putting green where the grass was fresh enough
for a ball not to roll too fast down the slightest slope.
Then together, including their obvious mother
– who was silent throughout, and it was not clear why –
they all went slowly on past a bandstand where
on Sundays the Subtopian Fusiliers
would often play the Merry Widow Waltz,
the theme tune of Ingmar Bergman's *Hamlet*.

Every bandsman was into promoting nostalgia
(*What else is left?* was the regimental motto)
and followed the injunction: *Think of beloved*
grandmothers and maiden aunts while you perform.
As receivers of treats and kindnesses with no idea
of their marriages, you adored them when you
were innocent children!
                              Then – *Time for our ice-creams!*
said the lady all at once, as I followed the group
to where I was going too, the Refreshment Room
(this was when it existed), and *Remember our custom!*
she "exclaimed" (enacting a favourite word).
What she meant was: *Take an ice-cream cornet,*
and break its end off to make a smaller cornet,
and with it scoop up some ice-cream so that you have
a tiny new cornet to give to a favourite friend.
It was not a routine that the mother liked at all,
not receiving many cornets of this kind.
Part of her silence consisted of not talking
to the lady throughout, not a word from her.
It was as if she thought her irrelevant
to whatever the afternoon could have been about
– like an irritation to be endured.
Was she stealing something from her by being there?
No giving or receiving went on between the two,
though the children did not notice.
                              It was a Thursday
in a dry late July, and with breezes on such days
early leaves will fall; so that the lady called
to the children suddenly, *Catch them, catch them!*
– in a high voice with a triumphant tone
that caused the mother to frown impatiently
as they ran round among the nearby plane trees
all catching and collecting, with the boy even
abandoning his horse to join in. *Now they won't have*
so many to sweep up come the autumn, she said,
out of breath and smiling, this just before her illness.
She seemed almost to feel it could make a difference.

■ Three memories of Ledbury Poetry Festivals, all clear and detailed. But the middle memory is alarming to recall.

The first: on 7th July 2002, my retained long list of poems for a reading to a large audience suggests I may have gone on too long. I see also that I read the opening pages of a recently published novel. Outside, afterwards, festival director Charles Bennett talks frantically into his walkie-talkie. About finding missing poets, or getting poets onto the right stage at the right time? Or getting them off the stage so the audience for the next readers can take their seats?

I have two appearances on 7th July 2005. I finish breakfast at a very good B&B and walk to the Market Theatre for the first: helping to launch a book on strokes by reading a contribution on that experience. 'Have you heard?' are the words greeting me. 'Heard?' It's the morning of the 7/7/05 bomb attacks in London. Events go ahead, but only after everyone with friends and relations have phoned there to establish their safety (I ring my son, safely at his place of work). Had I been coming to Ledbury that day instead of the day before I might have been at Edgware Road station... But on to 9th September 2009.

Eddie Linden and I are onstage for an hour's session we aren't sure will work: two poets with contrasting backgrounds and outlooks on poetry united by our dedication to the art and just hoping the microphones work. Somehow we move gently on from births in Glasgow and Catford through childhoods in poverty and respectability, and we contrast schools and work experiences, and talk friends in the poetry world, and let poems we have written on similar subjects take over – and a pleasant hour is up and no one has left yet. does Ledbury do that to audiences? [AB]

JOHN BURNSIDE

Midnight in Novosibirsk

– where, once, I dreamed
of waking in the chill
of springtime, with your arm
across my chest –
is 6 pm in London, where the rain
has just begun to fall, fat
herring-coloured drops
spotting the pavement
outside the budget hotel

where, last night, I dreamed of you
in Novosibirsk,
walking alone in snow, the birch woods
empty, but for the wind
and the blown ash of yesterday's fires
at the edge of town
where, last night, you dreamed
of horsewomen, tender and wild,
crossing the plain
in a ribbon of gun smoke and song.

CIARAN CARSON

Rain

(after Francis Ponge)

The rain, in the courtyard where I'm watching it
come down, comes down at many different rates of knot.
Its central zone is a finely woven curtain – sheer net, perhaps –
thinly broken, relentless in its fall, but
relatively slow, which must be down to the lightness
and size of its droplets, an ongoing, frail precipitation,
like real weather atomised.

Heavier and noisier the elemental drops
that fall close to hand to the walls to the left and right:
here the calibre of grains of wheat, there plump as peas,
elsewhere ample glassy marbles. Along window rail and sill
the rain washes horizontally, while clinging to
their undersides in rows of tetrahedral beads.

According to the whole surface of a little zinc roof
overhung by my lookout, it streams in a very fine sheet,
shimmering on account of the currents
variously created by the imperceptible undulations,

bumps and ripples of the metal blanketing;
and from the adjoining gutter, where it runs slowly
along with all the force of a low-gradient runnel, it suddenly
releases its flow in a long, perfectly vertical,
elegantly braided thread to the ground where
it shatters and spatters into brilliant glinting needles.

Each of its modes generates a particular tempo to which
a particular sonority responds. The whole ensemble pulses
like a complicated, living mechanism, as precise as it is
erratic, like a store of clocks whose springs depend on
the weight of a given mass of constantly condensing vapour.
The tinkling of vertical strings as they strike the ground,
gutters going glug-glug, dings, dongs and tiny gongs
resound and multiply in simultaneous concert, by no means
monotonous, and not without a certain fluid delicacy.

And in due course, as the springs run out of steam,
some of the waterwheels go on operating, though more slowly
and more slowly, until the mechanism ticks to a halt.
Then the sun comes out once more to wipe the slate clean;
the whole brilliant apparatus evaporates: it has rained.

KAYO CHINGONYI ■ ZAMBIA / UK

In Defence of Darkness

Drum-brush of fabric. The clink of a zip
on laminate floor. You step from a skirt
to the sound of the street outside swelling
with traffic, the sound of our breathing.

We've time to touch like we used to –
the harshness of the journey written
into the depth of a clinch. Chest to chest,
your head in the cleft of my breastbone.

Coconut Oil, laundry detergent, sweat,
dry shampoo, *Burberry Weekend*.
Garam Masala tang in the troublesome
hair inherited by our possible daughter.
I kneel, the better to drown in your scent.

Since I'm remembering this, or making it up,
there is only darkness; our bodies speaking.
Eat, your pelvis tells me. I eat – savouring
your aftertaste: tart but sweet, the inside

of a cheek, cured meat, a local delicacy.

TOM CHIVERS

Fallout

When you are shaking

   When you are shaking
  & we are holding on

    When you are shaking
with both hands on the kitchen worktop
    & we are holding on

   When we are holding on
     all three of us
     shaking with you
     trying to contain you

   When there's a stew on
     which you've cooked for us
       & you watch us eat it
     because that is something you can do for us

& the stew is rich & dark
you are no longer shaking
    but asleep in your chair
one half of your face collapsed
        like a riverbank
& I am walking into leaves
    & the city
filled up with rum & gravy

When there is metal between us
    solid metal & doors so thick
        you tell us we're in a fallout shelter
    & even the leaves on the ground are poisoned
        so I buy us a coffee
            & order a taxi
        from the special phone
            that dials the same voice every time
                & we wait in the comfy seats
            like a couple of guys going out
                for a walk

GILLIAN CLARKE

Eisteddfod of the Black Chair
(for Hedd Wyn, 1887-1917)

Robert Graves met him once,
in the hills above Harlech,
the shepherd poet,
the *awdl* and the *englyn* in his blood
like the heft of the mountain
in the breeding of his flock.

In a letter from France, he writes
of poplars whispering, the sun going down
among the foliage like an angel of fire.
and flowers half hidden in leaves
growing in a spent shell.
'Beauty is stronger than war.'

Yet he heard sorrow in the wind, foretold
blood in the rain reddening the fields
under the shadow of crows,
till he fell to his knees at Passchendaele,
grasping two fists-full of earth, a shell to the stomach
opening its scarlet blossom.

At the Eisteddfod they called his name three times,
his audience waiting to rise, thrilled,
to crown him, chair him,
to sing the hymn of peace,
not 'the festival in tears and the poet in his grave',
a black sheet placed across the empty chair.

BILLY COLLINS ■ USA

Our Poem

The choice of season is up to you, reader,
though autumn and winter are best for poetry
and you can decide the time of day –
not just my favorites, dawn or late afternoon –
and if you feel like it, mention the day of the week.

And what I was feeling at the time
I would leave up to you as well,
buoyant contentment in the shadow of mortality
being one of many options, the similarity
between the sugar of joy and the salt of sorrow another.

Whether I was sitting, standing, or lying
is another thing I place in your hands
without even mentioning a porch, a train window,
or a kitchen, all of which I find conducive to introspection.

Then there is the matter of what I was looking at –
also your decision, entirely your call.
The choices here can be overwhelming
in a world holding at least 10,000 things
so you might want to devote more time to that one.

You could decide upon a beach
and add a solitary swimmer, arm crooked above a wave,
a dog asleep on a towel, whatever you think fits.
The pen is in your hand. I'm not even here any more.

One last thing – I'd love to have a look at the results.
But not right now because right now
I'm watching a pair of swans floating
in winter's last remaining circle of open water.

You take the ball and run with it
and leave me to lean against this shore-anchored oak
at dusk on a Wednesday in early March.

■ The Ledbury Poetry Festival was a many-splendoured thing for me: a lively workshop, a sense of poetry in the air, a long delayed side-trip to Tintern Abbey, plus the scrambled eggs at that corner restaurant with cream and butter added were the best in the world! [BC]

DAVID CONSTANTINE

Fields

Ploughed, before sowing, one in the Cotswolds, the flints
Glinted and among them, dull, difficult to spot:
Small perfect lampshells, freed from the matrix, clean
And singular like the alive or dead today
At tidefall; sea-urchins, handy as slingstones
Their lovely petalling; many sharp belemnites.

Another under the olive trees at Gortys
In a breeze, in a watery dappling, the dry
Hard earth after the gush of poppies and thickly
Everywhere, easy to spot: four millenia
A stratum of sherds, warm krater handles, oh how
I wanted a girl's head lifted and the flute.

A third before Guillemont, ploughed, gently sloping
Quite without cover, in the deep chalk furrows
It was hard to walk, but the finds were evident:
A button, the shoe of a great shire horse, leather
Wire, iron, casings, lengths and splinters of bone
Eyes down, the stumbling men closer and closer.

■ About Ledbury, I'd just like to say that it is one of the two or three very best poetry festivals in the UK, the least mercantile, wholly there for the love of poetry, extraordinary in its yearly variety, in a town just made for easy meetings and conversation, in country I love because the hills are not far off. [DC]

WENDY COPE

Orb

An illuminated orb
against a black background –
the colour of flesh, with faint
red lines that could be rivers.

Not a planet in the night sky:
my eyeball
on the optician's screen.

It's beautiful. Just one small feature
of a mysterious universe
I'll never explore, packed neatly
in this soft container.

We know so little of ourselves,
and of each other – the working parts
we carry everywhere,

the darkness we scan
like astronomers, seeking
the half-forgotten stories of our lives.

JULIA COPUS

Grievers

At length we learned what it meant to "come to" grief.
As if grief lay in wait for us all along,
a barricade or boulder in the road.

What was it pulled us to it – led as we were
to its cold, stone smell, its granite skin?
We knew it by the way the light had shrunk
to a frayed corona; slowly, we understood
there was nothing to do but swallow it whole
and inch our way forward again. But to find we were able –
that was the miracle. It was as if the soul,
which has no definite shape, consisted simply
of a flexible cell wall, for the journey taught us
that in the face of grief the soul distorts
and forms a seal around the loss.
The bits we can't absorb we carry in us,
a lumpish residue. It is truly a wonder
we manage to move at all; let alone
as freely as this, with the ease at times
of our old and lighter selves. And when I say we…
Look out into the street – we are everywhere:
on bikes, at bus-stops, among the crowds
of those who have not happened yet on grief.
We steady our own like an egg in the dip of a spoon,
as far as the dark of the hallway, the closing door.
Some are there now, in the measling light
that gathers behind doors. We are catching our breath,
certain we won't be joining you again,
confounding ourselves at the last because we do.

LORNA CROZIER ■ CANADA

The Underworld

I

The River Styx has no beginning.
It's just a metaphor for grief.
But the dog is real. People like to tell you
their dog is a Rescue Dog.

This one isn't.
He's set his coat on fire.

II

Mother, mother, you say, hoping she'll appear.
You didn't know she had so much in her –
such anguish. So many damaged wings.

III

The poet said all wounds close at night.
They don't. There is the bird torn open.
There is the naked heart. The gash in the fir tree.
Perhaps it is morning here. Wait a few hours.
The sutures may happen. A bone-needle
threaded with an eternal sleeper's drool.

IV

Not as dark as you thought.
Something gives off a kind of light.
What makes you inconsolable is the silence.
No wind in leaves. No grass speaking.
The shadows are more than shadows.
There seems to be a lot of waiting.
Only one doctor and all these cities of the dead.

TADEUSZ DABROWSKI   ■ POLAND

Nothing was made

Here, where roe deer, black bears, squirrels and boar full
of eyes in front and behind go running across your
bedclothes, where you restlessly pace the length of superstores
that look forward to seeing you twenty-four hours a day,
ready to sell you six gallons of beer, a three-pound
bag of chips for two, a "party box" of condoms

in the largest size, a Batman costume deceptively
similar to the original, and even a night
shirt shaped like a rasher of bacon; where cars
as big as combines harvest your dream of escaping
into the backwoods, along with wild brutes and brutalised
people; where skipping along canals, you take the measure of time,
successive arousing and settings of the sun, you meet women
with tattoos on their irises and souls like Nagasaki
(following contact with the Fat Man) or the latest iPhone;
right here, half-way through your life – for you're always
half-way through – you suddenly hear the prices freeze,
the bellies of fridges and vagrants cease to rumble,
tumors and politicians no longer feel like multiplying
the obvious, the dead aren't anxious about their bank balance
standing in line for the cashier, tattoos erupt in the sky,
which closes its blind eye to the high jinks
of clouds and teenagers in student dorms, the assassin's
bullet hangs in mid-air and is not yet
lethal, a thought solidifying between synapses. And right here
poetry appears, and forces a stag to bolt
in front of the hood of your car, bids an apple break free
of its branch, the light to burgeon and burst the shell
of the night, a husband to think of his wife while
masturbating, airplanes to fly to, and ramblers to walk to their goal,
God to perform a few miracles, the liar to win another
election, the religious poet to write some good
verse. Nobody saw it. But without it, nothing was made
that was made.

(Hudson 2013)

translated from the Polish by Antonia Lloyd-Jones

FRED D'AGUIAR ■ GUYANA / UK/ USA

Transit Lounge

3AM enforced sleep, body a pretzel across partitioned seats,
I dream, retreat, moonwalk backwards away from all this,
Free in water, buoyed by salt, dreadlocks replace my bald
Head, tentacles of hair, widespread, moon-dance, spellbound,
Air pockets in my bones, adrift, looking up through liquid lens
At a vacuum of stars for any sign, please, about this puzzle pieces
Flesh stamped, tattoo-veined, pulse, gas, chemical mix, man,
Left to his own design, device, as if marrow could rudder
Bone craft to harbour, heel to instep to ball of footstep,
Hop and drop glide from one pothole to the next, empty
Plate skull stuck with brain food for thought some fool
Bought for a wink and nod, and *hey presto*, abracadabra,
Broke again, left to his own vice once more as push comes
To shovel rich pong, no ding, dung, for rich is as rich does.

Bam! She skips along with her Rapunzel hair, black,
Smile of a Mona, with teeth, charm in dimples, in her
Headlamps and her touch that turn bones to liquid,
Hot, oh gods, molten, so sky spits thunder, thrills light,
Days, nights, daze, nerves stretched, time just as elastic.
Turn, scan lounge, touch luggage, head down, off again,
This time my bald scalp shines crimson and I burn arctic,
Chased by a bear on skates, me running naked on water,
Don't ask me how, this is a transit lounge at 3, I am not my
Self, not now, when all I want is for Lennon to be true,
Just for a NY minute across all thirty-some cardinal points
With all skin peeled from bone and all bones scrubbed
By air in light spread equal on scales tipped with grime
Whose hurt, even here in this lounge, eases for a time.

AMIR DARWISH

■ SYRIA / UK

Fizzy Drink

Once near an Aleppo
Grocery store,
Bought a fizzy drink
Then Shock it.

Twenty years later,
I gaze into that bottle
On a window cell
Here in England.

Fearful to
Left the led,
Acknowledge
The crush.

Come whatever may,
Will open
The bottle
One day.

JIM DENING

A cold sun

A cold sun glances through the trees;
along the frosted track a fluffed-up robin
and his mate the blackbird scamper
towards their feast of a few crumbs.
What time of renewal is at hand?
The seeds have frozen in the cracked earth.

What promises, what mendacity have kept
the people quiet along their slippery streets?
Oh, we will see the season through,
with brave spirits and absurd jokes,
with our cocked heads and bright eyes,
with our mates we will see it through
as if we were all young together
and might yet lead flaming lives.

IMTIAZ DHARKER ■ PAKISTAN / INDIA / UK

Wolf, Words

In another room, the children are pigs.
You can hear them truffling behind sofas,
bumping chairs, snuffling round table-legs.

From the dregs of a story, the wolf
inks in, pulled to the sound of breathing,
drawn to the warm, the living,

rasping, *Let me in. Let me in.*
In their literal world, the children believe
the wolf is a wolf not a wolf made of words.

They make themselves small behind closed doors
in a house made of straw and a house made of sticks
and a house made of bricks, in a time

made of tricks. But the breath of the wolf
is the breath of the world. It blows a flurry
of straw, a volley of twigs, a fall

of rubble down on the pigs
who come squealing, squalling out of the storm
to a house made of words. This.

Scratching at walls, something is out there,
ever and after, something that howls.
What outcast word, what unhoused soul?

ISOBEL DIXON

■ SOUTH AFRICA / UK

Late Knowledge

I have forgotten the Periodic Table of the Elements,
apart from the famous few
and the look of the waxy scroll of text
unfurled against the science lab's wall,
Earth's Ten Commandments graphed in code.
I went with my father in the night as a little girl,
when he was setting up experiments,
sat long and studied it, in fascinated ignorance.

And I have forgotten basic chemistry,
apart from the dancing fizz of phosphorus
and the day my father's sulphurous show and tell
expelled him and the Standard Nines, out
to the quad in search of air. The same quad where
I watched the senior girls rehearse their witchiness
around mysterious brew – their fire burn
and cauldron bubble scorched into my brain.

Goniwe, like my father, taught, not far away,
but then I didn't know his name; Cradock
just another dusty settlement, minor satellite
to our own, all unrest pressed out to the margins –
his Lingelihle, our Umasizakhe stirring up
a history not taught in my calm classrooms.
And he was sent to prison in the town
where I was born, the Communist suppressed

and then so inconveniently returned.
I have forgotten, if I ever read,
what the *Eastern Province Herald* said
about their disappearances – Sparrow Mkhonto,
Fort Calata, Sicelo Mhlauli, Matthew Goniwe,
the Cradock Four. If they printed anything at all
until their permanent removal from society
(that terrible permission from on high) was clear.

Who thought to bring the telephone wire?
(Strangled, stabbed and shot – so dangerous
one killing wasn't death enough?)
Who poured the petrol on each face
to sear away the individual flesh?
What did they talk of while the bodies burned?
And which one cut off Matthew's hands?
What calculation was this and what settled score?

In the lab, my father readied for his class;
I watched Lady Macbeth try to erase the marks.
But I drive now with those men, Olifantshoek
to Bluewater Bay – the threatening
and the defiant, frightened for their lives.
That road, the darkest pass. These are the nights
we've no will to recall, but must, how
something evil always in among us was.

In memory of Matthew Goniwe, Sparrow Mkhonto, Fort Calata & Sicelo Mhlauli

MAURA DOOLEY

A bunch of consolation
(Adrian Mitchell)

You think they'll always be there,
(the ones who always have been).

They showed you the way,
not their way
but how to find your own
(and what to say),
sweeping the path of leaves

or snow

but then *they* leave, they go,
before you were ready
(how could you ever be ready?)
to wonder, wondering,   .
what have you learned exactly?
To love, to speak up, to hold steady.

Hold steady.

MARK DOTY

■ USA

In Two Seconds
(Tamir Rice, 2002–2014)

the boy's face
climbed back down the twelve-year tunnel

of its becoming, a charcoal sunflower
swallowing itself. Who has eyes to see,

or ears to hear? If you could see
what happens fastest, unmaking

the human irreplaceable, a star
falling into complete gravitational

darkness from all points of itself, all this:

the held loved body into which entered
milk and music, honeying the cells of him:

who sang to him, stroked the nap
of the scalp, kissed the flesh-knot

after the cord completed its work
of fueling into him the long history

of those whose suffering
was made more bearable

by the as-yet-unknown of him,

playing alone in some unthinkable
future city, a Cleveland,

whatever that might be.
Two seconds. To elapse:

the arc of joy in the conception bed,
the labor of hands repeated until

the hands no longer required attention,
so that as the woman folded

her hopes for him sank into the fabric
of his shirts and underpants. Down

they go, swirling down into the maw
of a greater dark. Treasure box,

comic books, pocket knife, bell from a lost cat's collar,
why even begin to enumerate them

when behind every tributary
poured into him comes rushing backward

all he hasn't been yet. Everything
that boy could have thought or made,

sung or theorised, built on the quavering
but continuous structure

that had proceeded him sank into
an absence in the shape of a boy

playing with a plastic gun in a city park
in Ohio, in the middle of the afternoon.

When I say *two seconds*, I don't mean the time
it took him to die. I mean the lapse between

the instant the cruiser braked to a halt
on the grass, between that moment

and the one in which the officer fired his weapon.
The two seconds taken to *assess the situation*.

And though I believe it is part
of the work of poetry to try on at least
the moment and skin of another,

but for this hour I respectfully decline.

I refuse it. May that officer
be visited every night of his life
by an enormity collapsing in front of him

into an incomprehensible bloom,
and the voice that howls out of it.

If this is no poem then...

But that voice – erased boy,
beloved of time, who did nothing
to no one and became

nothing because of it – I know that voice
is one of the things we call poetry.

It isn't to his killer he's speaking.

CAROL ANN DUFFY

22 Reasons for the Bedroom Tax

Because the Badgers are moving the goalposts.
The Ferrets are bending the rules.
The Weasels are taking the hindmost.
The Otters are downing tools.

The Hedgehogs are changing the game-plan
The Grass-snakes are spitting tacks.
The Squirrels are playing the blame-game.
The Skunks are twisting the facts.

The Pole-cats are upping the ante.
The Foxes are jumping the gun.
The Voles are crashing the party.
The Stoats are dismantling the Sun.

The Rabbits are taking the biscuit.
The Hares are losing the plot.
The Eagles are kicking the bucket.
The Rats are joining the dots.

The Herons are throwing a curveball.
The Shrews are fanning the flames.
The Field mice are sinking the 8-ball.
The Swans are passing the blame.

And the Pheasants are draining the oil from the tank –
but only the Bustards have broken the bank.

IAN DUHIG

The Passion of the Holly
(AIR: The Sans Day Carol)

We're the Sans Day carolers who call once a year;
if we're sans bread and sans brass, we are not sans care,
for the coming of Jesus, born poor to be king
and the passion of the holly at Christmas we sing.

O the holly bore a berry as white as a bone,
for we sing of one new life but many more gone,
so we sing for those grieving as all theirs who died,
whether Christian or not at this cold Christmastide.

But the holly bore a berry as green as new grass,
as Our Lady bore Jesus who died on the cross,
and if summer seems laid in the sepulchre's night –
no dark hold's so strong it's not broken by light.

When the holly bore a berry as black as a mine,
we lit thirty-three candles like Christ's years, a sign;
for poor miners give daylight their living to make,
and some sacrificed more when the holly wore black.

Now the holly bears a berry as Christ's blood it's red,
for the Christ-child means good that can rise from the dead;
and much sharper than holly was Jesus's crown,
and yet he was raised up and Lord Satan cast down.

O our holly and its berry were soon turned to dust,
as were we who in singing and kindness put trust;
and yet though we sing now to you from the grave,
you can hear us because we are singing of love.

■ This poem first appeared in the Guardian of 17/12/2010 and alludes to the rescue of the Chilean miners among other things. It was part of a commission by Carol Ann Duffy to update Christmas carols and it reminds me of Ledbury because it struck me as at the centre of so many traditions as well as being involved in the Industrial Revolution – I think of the navvies in Masefield's poems. I have many warm memories of Ledbury and one of utter astonishment which I describe now: when I came down to be poet in residence a while ago, I'd written most of a sequence of sonnets for the occasion which began from the City of Troy not far from Shandy Hall in North Yorkshire, one of Shakespeare's 'quaint mazes in the wanton green' from *A Midsummer Night's Dream*. Various developments suggested themselves from this, however, I needed inspiration for a concluding sonnet when I wandered up the High Street to where I was being put up, ideally something that would link the sequence back to the maze – this sort of thing was buzzing in my mind when I pushed open the gate into where I would be staying and saw an exact, life-size copy of the Yorkshire City of Troy in the garden. This experience set me off on another trail I won't go into but the surprise of seeing a form I thought lodged in my brain laid out on the wanton green was magical and I can't imagine it happening to me anywhere except at Ledbury. That sense of the forms of country traditions reasserting themselves with sudden relevance lay behind the approach I took to writing 'The Passion of the Holly'. [ID]

HELEN DUNMORE

Ten Books

Jacketless, buckled, pressed from the voyage,
Ten books that once were crated to America
And back again,
That have known the salt sea's swing under them,
Oil stink, the deep throb of the engines
And quick hands putting them back on the shelves.

Spines torn, the paper wartime, the Faber
Font squarish and the dates in Roman:
The Waste Land and other poems,
Poems Newly Selected, Siegfried Sassoon –
How that name conjured with me
As a soldier kicked at a dead man.

MacNeice, freckled with brown
From many damps in many different houses.
On the inner page, under my father's autograph
An early flourish of blue crayon
Where I scribbled a figure so primitive
There are not even legs for it to walk upon.

Bowed, chipped, darkening, edge-worn
Sunned, loose, fading
Binding copy, reading copy, shaken:
Ten books that I have taken.
From the balcony on an August morning
I see the rest fly to the tip lorry

Where the sofa for a moment reposes
Legs in the air, grinning.
It is soaked through with music
But nothing will save it.
Behind it the sea makes the usual silveriness,
The café opens and the bikes whizz

From end to end of the promenade.
Meanwhile in my father's hand, a quotation
On the title page of Herbert Read's
Thirty-Five Poems: 'I absorbed Blake,
His strange beauty, his profound message,
His miraculous technique, and to emulate

Blake was to be my ambition
And my despair...' (Faber and Faber,
24 Russell Square.) I see my own hands
Smooth and small as they are not now
Lifting, turning, 'I am amazed
To find how much I owe to him.'

■ Ledbury Poetry Festival stores up the essence of poetry throughout its packed, intense and sunlit days. [HD]

DOUGLAS DUNN

Botanics

Multicoloured clothespegs on the line
Are tiny tropical birds hanging upside down.
Their songs are all imaginary.
The tree peony's a candelabrum,
Botanical flame-holder. Maples speak
Native American languages, a eucalypt
Aboriginal Australian, Pieris
A secret tongue of the forest. Magnolia –
Which I don't have although a neighbour does –
Discusses Mississippi in a Dixie drawl.
Ranks of *en garde* gladioli speak
Byzantine Greek, roses Babylonish
And other floral tongues, while quince
Talks Arabic, and an azalea is
A chatterbox in Hindi and Chinese.
Lilies whisper across continents
In secret, erotic dialects
That baffle botanical philologists.
Crab-apple – good for jelly – it speaks
Weathered and salty Atlantic lingos,
Survivors' syntax. Spare a thought
For currants, strawberry, raspberry, gooseberry,
Indigenous desserts, mother-made jam,
For lilacs, elder, and the evergreens,
For the big library of tree-poetry
In botany's symphonic chorus.

Thunder raining poison

a whisper arrives. *two thousand. two thousand or more*. did you hear it?
          that bomb. the torture of red sand turning green
                the anguish of earth turned to glass
          did you hear it? *two thousand. two thousand or more*
          yams cremated inside the earth. poison trapped
                in glass like a museum. did you hear it?
                two thousand. two thousand or more
                    tears we cried for our Land
     for the fear you gave us, for the sickness and the dying
                two thousand years of memory here
                two thousand. two thousand or more
peaceful place this place. happy place till you come with your bombs
          you stole our happiness with your poison ways
                    you stole our stories
                two thousand. two thousand or more
          our people gone missing. did you hear it?
          where's my grandfather? you seen him?
          where's my daughter? you seen her?
          Mummy! You seen my mum? Dad!
                two thousand. two thousand or more
          times I asked for truth. do you know where they are?
                two thousand. two thousand or more
     trees dead with arms to the sky. all the birds missing. no bird
                        song here
          just stillness. like a funeral. two thousand or more
                a whisper arrives. did you hear it?
                two thousand. two thousand or more
it sounds like glass. our hearts breaking. but we are stronger than that
     we always rise us mob. *two thousand. two thousand or more*
          you can't break us. we not glass. we're people!
                two thousand. two thousand or more
          our Spirit comes together. we make a heart
     did you see it? in the fragments. it's there in the glass
                two thousand. two thousand or more

our hearts grow as we mourn for our Land
it's part of us. we love it. poisoned and all

■ This poem is a response to the installation *Thunder raining poison* created
by Kokatha glass artist Yhonnie Scarce. It is a statement about the impact of
atomic bomb testing on our traditional Lands at Maralinga in South Australia,
by the British Govt. during the 1940-1960s. [ACE]

JONATHAN EDWARDS

Servant Minding a Seat for his Master Before a Performance of *The Rivals*, Covent Garden Theatre, 1775

I do what I'm told, me. What does sir need?
Some pleb to take a load off, guard your seat,
to sit right back and put his paid-for feet

up, three hours, four, sat on your hands –
guv'nor, I'm your man. Sir, master, boss,
it might seem wasted time but it's no loss –

my master is a god to me. The one
thing that bothers me is Gossip John
who minds the next seat over, passes hours,

now whispering about our master's trips
after dark to some house on the docks,
now of our lady's preference for cloth

to silk, or how she passes like the breeze
through servants' rooms which echo with her squeals.
It's all a gas for John to sell or share

their weaknesses, their joys. I wouldn't dare –
he spills the beans and turns to me and winks;
I blush and turn away and bow my head

and say the thing that's often been heard said
about my master by the Duke of Gloucester –
his dignity, his wit. It's a relief

when master comes, leading his frilly daughter.
Now nobody would see, we're up so quick,
the subtle look that flicks from her to me,

as master's arse slips snug onto the seat
I've warmed for him. I've never seen a play,
but as I walk away from this performance,

the sound of clapping, listen, dogs my heels.

■ Ledbury Poetry Festival formed an enormous part of my poetic education,
both through the poets it allowed me to see read, and through its excellent
and supportive one-to-one tutorial sessions. After going every year for the
best part of a decade, to have my poem recognised in the competition and to
be on the other side of things, reading in the legendary Burgage Hall, where
I'd seen so many events, was a truly awesome experience. [JE]

RHIAN EDWARDS

The Gulls Are Mugging

The gulls are mugging the scholars again;
stalking lunches on parade, making nests
of hapless human scalps. It is then they unhinge
the jaws, snatch the booty whole, broad daylight
poaching from your unwelcoming hand.

Don't let the dove feathers fool you,
the slapstick march or the witless China
doll eyes. They could shawl their plumage
around you in a burlesque stole, smokescreen
you away into the perfect vanishing act.

They can dip bread in the ocean, bait fish
into their tricking beaks. They have no qualms
pecking chunks from a whale hide when it surfaces
to breathe. They mate for life to rival the romance
of the swan, taking turns to brood until the chicks fledge.

Far from birdbrained, this is organised crime;
these rogue pickpocketers, mob raiders, white-suited
butchers. And they have all the elements covered:
these camp criers of the skies, fishwives of the seas,
unpacified foul mouths of this concrete square.

KRISTIINA EHIN ■ ESTONIA

'This world...'

This world in the shape of a shopping trolley
will roll down to the shore of the sea one day
where I sit on a stone and draw a stamp of me
to put in a bottle and send on its way.

And in a hundred years on a faraway isle,
where the phone rebels and Skype is weak,
you would find the serpentine arches of my eyes
in a fishing net cast out into the sea.

I'd appear before you as sudden as lightning
and naked as the moon. Now pull the cork!
I'd blind you from the bottle like the sun shining –
the stamp's to be drawn so it makes its mark,

reminding you piercingly of the time when
a thousand years ago on the same shore
as a lover you gave me the very thing
that can never be taken back any more.

How night gorges… Our times are a sight to see –
wormeaten remnants of images of beauty.
This world in the shape of a shopping trolley
will be smashed all to bits one day

here against this stone that has no wishes,
with the shallow sea all around for aeons.
As those condemned to death, who have no riches,
the blood pulsed within us.

translated from the Estonian by Ilmar Lehtpere

MENNA ELFYN

Gyrru trwy Gariad
(i G.F. am ei gwaith dros heddwch)

Ar fore cynta'r rhyfel prynodd feic,
anghenraid i heddychwraig, meddai,
un main i sleifio drwy'r holl lonydd cefn
heb faricêd. Wrth agor eu llenni pren
gwelodd swyddog yn arthio ar ddau lanc
mewn lifrai a'u gwaith blêr ar wifren bigog

yn tasgu llid. Mewn byddin rhaid talu parch,
mesur manwl gywir yw'r drefn. A dyna a wnaeth
drwy fynd rhag blaen yn slei bach i'r siop
feiciau, carden credyd fel arf mewn llaw;
hyhi, yr unig gwsmer yno'n fore am 9.
Cael hwyl anfarwol yno wrth ddewis gêrs,
dal gafael â'r llyw mewn dwy law;
dewis un â'i basged a'i wagle hael.
A'r perchennog? Roedd wrth ei fodd,
rhodd ostyngiad da gan ddweud –
ar adeg fel hon mae eisie poced ddofn.

Dydd bythgofiadwy ydoedd. Beic fflamgoch
yn belydr o bleser yn erbyn wyneb bwrlwcs
yr awyr. Ddyddiau wedyn, aeth y rhestr
yn hwy: y gorweddog a'r anabl a'r sawl
heb allu ciwio am gyfreidiau: wyau a llaeth:
ei pharseli o heddwch oedd eu bara beunyddiol.

Rhyfel deuddeng niwrnod a gafwyd. A'r beic?
Bellach ar orwedd yn rhwd i gyd.
Ei medal? Anhysbys wrth gwrs. Un heb chwennych
dim oll ond y chwedl fel y gall rhywun yrru
trwy gariad ac ennill y dydd yn y ddinas nwydus
lle bydd defod y llu wrth groesi'r bont yn Ljubljana
yn cusanu fforddolion eraill ar eu taith.

Fforddolion? Teithwyr ar droed. Weiren bigog,
baricêds. Sbocsen o adain olwyn sy'n stond.
Yn fud hyd yn oed. Fel y dywedwn ffordd hyn,
      yr un hen, hen wahaniaeth.

Love rides high

(for G.F. for her quiet acts during the Balkans war)

The day the war started she bought a bike.
It's what a peacemaker needs, she said: lean
enough to steal through lanes with no barricade.
Opening her shutters that morning she saw
an officer bellowing at two lads in uniform
for sloppy work on barbed wire. War after all

requires a duty of care. Precision in practice.
So she followed their lead, sneaking
into a bike shop armed only with her credit card:
the sole customer this 9 a.m.
Had the time of her life,
choosing the right gears, the handlebars:
just so for holding baskets abrim.

The owner, bemused was so pleased –
gave her a discount. In times like these
he said, we all need a deep pocket.

That was a day to remember, her bike, blood red,
and a sunburst of delight at the sky's
stony face. Days later, she lengthened her list:
those bedridden, unable to queue for milk, eggs,
her little parcels of peace, their daily bread.

The twelve-day war they called it then. Her bike
now rested and rusty, was her badge of honour once,
anon. Of course. She who'd want none but the tale
of how love can make one ride high and dry
in that city of passion where people as they cross
the bridge in Ljubljana kiss all passers by.

Passers by? Today wayfarers on foot. Barbed wire,
barricades? 'Spoke' another word which turns us dumb,
stock still. As we say far away, it's all the same difference.

translated from the Welsh by the author

MARTÍN ESPADA   ■ USA

How We Could Have Lived or Died This Way

> Not songs of loyalty alone are these,
> But songs of insurrection also,
> For I am the sworn poet of every dauntless rebel the world over.
>
> WALT WHITMAN

I see the dark-skinned bodies falling in the street as their ancestors fell
before the whip and steel, the last blood pooling, the last breath spitting.
I see the immigrant street vendor flashing his wallet to the cops,
shot so many times there are bullet holes in the soles of his feet.

I see the deaf woodcarver and his pocketknife, crossing the street
in front of a cop who yells, then fires. I see the drug raid, the wrong
door kicked in, the minister's heart seizing up. I see the man hawking
a fistful of cigarettes, the cop's chokehold that makes his wheezing
lungs stop wheezing forever. I am in the crowd, at the window,
kneeling beside the body left on the asphalt for hours, covered in a sheet.

I see the suicides: the conga player handcuffed for drumming on the
        subway,
hanged in the jail cell with his hands cuffed behind him; the suspect
        leaking
blood from his chest in the back seat of the squad car; the 300-pound boy
said to stampede barehanded into the bullets drilling his forehead.

I see the coroner nodding, the words he types in his report burrowing
into the skin like more bullets. I see the government investigations stacking,
words buzzing on the page, then suffocated as bees suffocate in a jar. I see
the next Black man, fleeing as the fugitive slave once fled the slave-catcher,
shot in the back for a broken tail light. I see the cop handcuff the corpse.

I see the rebels marching, hands upraised before the riot squads,
faces in bandannas against the tear gas, and I walk beside them unseen.
I see the poets, who will write the songs of insurrection generations unborn
will read or hear a century from now, words that make them wonder
how we could have lived or died this way, how the descendants of slaves
still fled and the descendants of slave-catchers still shot them, how we
        awoke
every morning without the blood of the dead sweating from every pore.

A Question for My Dead

I'm alone in the house and suddenly feel
the need to phone my mother. But it's decades
since she died – and I don't remember ever
having this urge before. Something altered.
Now, for the first time in thirty years
she wanted her daughter, and I want to talk
to them: mother, father, brother, husband –
all my dead. But what do I want to ask them?

Like a glass of water, darkened by one drop
of ink, I am suffused by unexpected thoughts.
Their realm and my world have no connection.
They have forgotten almost everything.
I look into my mother's eyes – they are calm
and seem paler, her gaze is barely focussed
but she is smiling; all of them are smiling.
As far as I can judge, they are happy –

although I'm not certain that they recognise me.
And where exactly are we? Is this puffy
stuff the floor of Heaven? Now I notice:
the four are dressed in suspiciously similar
clothes, which could be robes, and those books
they hold look holy. Then they start to sing:
a sanctimonious droning counterpoint.
It makes me anxious. Might I be dead as well?

I look down at an unfamiliar garment
(I seem to be wearing a nightdress):
does this mean that I've joined the family choir?
I love them, and I'm old enough, for sure –
nonetheless, it's far too soon to die.
At last I know the question, but realise
they'll never give an answer. The phone rings.
I'm awake, at my desk. My throat tightens.

Clever and Cold

It's hard being clever and cold.
And I should know. Jack Frost came
to my childhood window one night and told
me: *Look, from now on things won't be the same.*

Its great stillness is not merely a pose.
Not coming in from the cold, but cold coming in.
I try to keep warm but ever since
our little mind-to-heart, I've known
cold's wider intelligence.

How all days should be crystal days.
You can see cold for yourself at work
in the shapes it makes
out of any January park:
fangs on the lip of the slide; a lid for the lake.

The sky is thinking hard before it snows.
You can see how frost hides from the sun,
keeping itself to the shadows
of walls and hedges. It has a mind of its own.
The sun can't have everything its own way.

These are some of the things cold knows.

Ask her

Ask her what she knows about the dawn of the lakes. Ask about
the roe deer's anxiety and the anxiety of noxious vermin. Ask
about the smell of timber and the longing of the milestones. Ask
her if the constellations of her childhood's starry skies have changed.
Ask if her body has been formed from this earth, if its pleasure
and sorrow are tied to its barrenness or fertility. Ask which songs
have shaped her hearing, which worn fabrics her hands have
touched before your skin. Ask what it means to belong, what
she'd forsake to ensure her belonging. Ask her which enemies
she's been forced to defend and which friends she's betrayed. Ask
her how it feels to lie next to someone who can sing the lullabies
she once fell asleep to. Ask her what death means to someone
who has a grave to go to. Ask her which trees she has cried next
to and how knowing their names affected her crying. Ask how it
feels to see yourself in someone's face and to know that face to be
valuable and meaningful. Ask if she's had to spurn something
only to be forced down on her knees in front of it. Ask her what
seasonal changes mean for someone who doesn't believe they're
only temporarily there. Ask about the holidays and sick days. Ask
if she wants witnesses to what you do with each other. Ask about
the lace tablecloths in the linen cupboard, about the heirlooms
within the heirlooms. Ask what it means to eat with the same
cutlery your ancestors scraped the same china with. Ask her who
taught her which mushrooms to be wary of, which woods to go
to. Ask who told her years of snow, fruit will grow, and that after
rain comes sunshine. Ask how she understood the difference
between bogs and swamps, between mittens and gloves, rule and
exception, dog and hound, bed rockers and bed legs. Ask her if
she will remember you as a stranger.

translated from the Swedish by Pamela Robertson-Pearce

VICKI FEAVER

Pugilist

Uncle who was killed in the War;
whose boxing gloves, stitched
from padded orange leather,
were stored in the cupboard
above my bed; who haunted

our house, making my father
feel guilty for not fighting
and dying and stopping
my mother and grandmother
from ever being happy.

On Remembrance Day,
when they sat behind green
velvet curtains, watching
a tiny black-and-white telly
and weeping as poppy wreaths

were laid on the cenotaph,
I sneaked out of the lounge
to dance on the lawn, paper poppy
pinned in my hair, leaping
and twirling in frosty grass.

That night, Uncle Jack
appeared in my dream –
jigging from foot to foot,
throwing punches at me
with bunched orange fists.

I woke with a nosebleed:
a flow of scarlet drops
soaking my pillow and sheets
and an old towel and half-
filling the blue kitchen bowl.

■ I remember having a really lovely time. I stayed for a couple of nights and had time to meet and eat and talk with the other poets. Often festivals only put you up for a night and you feel rather deflated on the way home. [VF]

ELAINE FEINSTEIN

The Last Trick of Harry Houdini

Driven to stunt after stunt:
   handcuffed in water,
buried underground

you would emerge triumphant.
   Cops double-locked their cells
but you broke out. Rivals

without your ingenuity,
   never collected that ten
thousand dollars you laid down.

You shook off any claim
   to supernatural powers,
artifice was the game,

trained lungs, hard muscles,
   and an athlete's discipline
underpinned your puzzles.

Heroic: a dead Rabbi's son,
   who poured gold coins
into a mother's apron.

You were invited into Royal palaces.
   A friend of Conan Doyle –
whose wife wrote spirit messages –

you went to visit stylish mediums,
   and were dismayed
to see through all the mysteries displayed.

It became a crusade. At seances
    which banned your attendance
you would use disguise. Or hired spies.

Newspapers ran your stories.
    One spirit guide
foretold your death – this you defied.

But were you wondering when you left
    a secret code word
with your wife, was it so absurd,

to imagine, once outside the town glare
    of being alive,
spirits becoming visible there

like stars on a clear night?
    And if anyone could break out
from an after-world, surely you might.

The thousands of fans at your funeral
    half-expected an escape – as if
for you death could never be final,

there had to be one last trick, yet afraid
    a lintel would suddenly crack,
and some fearful window break open –

until that Wand of Rosewood was broken
    by the President of Magicians,
with due ceremony, over the silent coffin.

JAMES FENTON

The Revenant

Why do you come a-tapping at the window
And wailing to me from the ice and snow?
You gave me to believe you were my lover.
You left me many friendless months ago.

You promised me a mirror from the city.
And seven scarlet ribbons for my hair.
Then you were gone, a-whistling down the valley
Driving your goats to sell at the Easter Fair.

You promised we'd be married in the summer.
The summer's come and gone, long time ago.
Why do you come a-tapping at the window
And wailing to me from the ice and snow.

He answers:

My love, my love, I did as I had promised.
I took my goats to sell at the Easter Fair.
But there were press-gangs placed throughout the city
And officers in every tavern there.

ROY FISHER

A Garden Leaving Home

One after another the windows that made it gave up looking.
The monitors cut out. No dashes for freedom:
there's always management. The sky
that had cared for the acre since the ocean receded
began taking it back again without comment.

Over a bank where nine
tall old native cherries had oozed, split
and tottered down to pulp the stretch of air
where years of magpies bungled their nests
kept not a memory of all that racket.

The plot filling up fast with curved shapes,
some very small, some moving; brambles
arching above themselves and breaking in waves

down inside the boundary wall. And above,
the patch where design had planted saplings at random
to develop the pretence of a little wood – rowan, field maple, hazel,
goat willow, crab, walnut, sloe – had become
the little wood.

S.J. FOWLER

Son of Ships

In this region of the new world
there exists but one man.
Though those that are born in ships
surround him,
and there must be a second, or third,
to have seen him,
he remains, alone, by order,
sliced white,
bound into skeletons.

One can live as a beggar, he says, while walking a king.
There are risks to the night not mentioned, or noticed.
Seven chambers, by seven chambers. Multiplying.
Mathematics on a page,
(rather than in the mind, or within a machine).
A doctor's report that is difficult to read
for a reason that is difficult to remember.
A kind of fame possible, only granted
when the one last man is discovered beyond Palermo.

We do not dare to state that we are simple.
The sea seems wider as we view it from the deck.
Or the neck of a river that keeps breeding.
The walk continues, only with music now.
        Honoris Causa in Jerusalem,
                possible sums of the numbers 8, 1 and 9, given twice.

There are duels, intruders, old ladies.
Houses, full of books, burning down.
There is a shadow so black
that it stretches ministers into poodles,
and poets into novelists.

The letters, arranged as poems,
attempt to live as Buenos Aires.
They fail with some skill,
and are better for the apology.
A soul's core, walking, writing,
a streetwalker in the innocent sense.
A single man, huge in a city,
small in the world.

ANGELA FRANCE

Cold Comfort

There is a comfort in shortening days,
in dark-at-five and damp roads shining.
Rain on the window whispers permission
to bolt the door and let the curtains sigh
along the rail. Outside, the pressure's low
and the moon's demands are muffled
in cloud. A rose bush, straggled with age,
taps at the glass and an ill-fitted door
knocks a little, now and again.
It's not quite cold enough to light the fire
but I'll do it anyway, lay the kindling
across paper, rattle coal from the scuttle,
wait for the crackle and draw. Nothing
is happening, no one is calling
and I'm glad of the night, the rain.

■ I go to Ledbury every year to recharge; it's so good for me to be in a place
where everyone understands that poetry matters. [AF]

ANNIE FREUD

Cobra Mist

Why did Cobra Mist never work as it should
and why were its defects so difficult to cure?
Some say it was jammed by the radio hams
filling the sky with their endless clutter;
and while *they* blamed the Russian Woodpeckers,
we put it down to the Rendlesham UFO
and others speculated in the gaps.
The sea's a great amplifier.

Valliants, Victors, Vulcans, Sopwiths and Sperrins –
all flew here and dropped their bombs
and even the bombs had names –
Blue Peacock, Blue Streak, Blue Danube,
Yellow Sun, Brown Bunny, Red Beard, Violet Club –
and were subject to stress and strain, like us.

FORREST GANDER   ■ USA

Evaporation: a Border History

Paisanos they call
            roadrunners, brothers of the land. A dozen
Mexican corpses maroon
                    under desert sun.
            In cottonwoods by the river,
zone-tailed hawks squeal. Visible
            from the air, the craquelure of
an abandoned runway
                            overlies
                    toxic waste and unexploded munitions.

Bordered by purple and yellow
bloomstalks: lechuguilla.
Volcanic chimneys up-thrust
from barren flats. Agleam
in a basalt outcrop, fist-size
feldspar crystals. The old raiding trails
from Comancheria converge
in a path packed by hoof prints.

Alarming ki-dear ki-dear of a
Cassin's kingbird on the
barbed fence. 150 miles
surveilled by a white aerostat
shaped like a whale. Between those peaks
sits Panther Laccolith. Both vaqueros
staked-out naked, left screaming on a live ant hill.
Female katydid waving her foreleg tympanum
at the stridulating males. The fine-
grained intrusion that veined the mountain
also silled Paint Gap Hill.
His horse quivers in agony, pinned to the ground by a lance.
Hovering over the field, a flock of crested flycatchers.
The border patrol dog lifts its leg
at the tire of the Skywagon. Coachwhip
fences parallel the dirt way. Chihuahua
Trail following Alameda Creek. They call it
horse-crippler cactus.

Vietnam-era seismic probes
buried across private lands. Lava rock rims the sides.
Give it a break, mockingbird.
El Despoblado. Giant yucca and bunch grass.
And what ventures into the afternoon heat? Only Pharoah ants.
Only the insulated darkling beetle.
On either side of the pavement, magnetic sensors
record movement and direction. Evening
cicadas eclipse tree crickets.
A thousand head of cattle

driven below the trachyte hoodoos. It nibbles
a prickly pear. Cottontail at dusk.
        Human contraband at dusk. Famous
    for their dwarf fauna, these fossil beds. Depositions of
      carnage, catches
          of light. The legacy
     mission. A carcass of the
       the unspeaking
           speaking.

■ Ledbury, the great long runs through the woods and past the French farm
to the sign that says HOPE END, gathering with others from everywhere on
the wobbly floor in the wonderful ancient communal space, Gōzō Yoshimasu
hammering a copper scroll and chanting in the Burgage Hall and our loveliest
of hosts, Chris and Bella Johnson. Ah. [FG]

AZITA GHAHREMAN   ■ IRAN / SWEDEN

The Boat That Brought Me

Behind these eyes that look like mine
old names are fading away, the past lies crumpled in my clenched fist –
a coppery bird in coppery wind,
this vast place has covered me from head to toe.

I am not stripped of word and thought
but sometimes what I want to say gets lost
like a moon smudged with cloud, or when I splutter on a drink.
My tongue trips up when I speak of that journey
though the blood in my veins felt the truth of death.
As I traced my footsteps through the tracery of my old language
Summer whispered to me
and my frozen fingers began to put out shoots
even as I began to love the cold ebb and flow of tides.

Sometimes I miss
the boat that brought me here,
now that I am witness to the icy eyes of a Swedish winter,
under these tired old clouds,
while that suitcase still holds a patch of the sky-blue me.

translated from the Farsi by Maura Dooley & Elhum Shakerifar

VONA GROARKE

This Being Still

I

With the dog's head on my foot, asleep,
it seems wrong to move.

She is getting old, doddery,
walks into doors and stumbles off kerbs,
feels her way by the edge of my voice.

I have brought her to an island
of cropped light and few words,
her silence just as diffuse as my own.

She keeps close into me.

It is a small gift to the world,
I reckon, this our being still.

II

In no time, at the clatter of a winter bird
or my book falling or the heat kicking in,

she will rise to the surface
of the last of day

and I will meet her milky gaze
to wonder what I wanted

to begin with.

PHILIP GROSS

The Day of the Things
(for R.S.)

The day came, as it had to, when the things
reclaimed themselves. An empty room,
open-plan, glimpsed from the train,
one table at a slant

as if a shaft of light had placed it... All the years
we'd been drawing them out, into
ourselves, as dreams, goods,
meanings, wants,

reversed. In the backwash, at first, we fell mute:
daily Dave, beside me at his tablet
on the 8:15, stone-motionless,
the screen blank

and his mirror image pixelating, fading in.
Then he was nothing but his headphones.
Children, they went lightly.
By their bunks,

a games console with gravitas, Lego
like Stonehenge, the parents' panic
from mobile to mobile an on-
vibrate quiver and moan

like wood doves… I could only be glad
for next-door Reg when his Bentley,
waxed bright as a conker,
came into its own.

Hush fell. Chill atria became cathedrals.
An empty carafe stood amply in
for a whole committee.
But how to decide

now which, was it that Le Creuset tureen
I'd married or that flick of her brush
or her glasses or… everything?
And what could I

be, still here, but the rough-scuffed notebook
I never owned wholly, with this seeping
in, this wilderment of ink,
this tanglewood

of word, root, tendril, from which why
would I wish to emerge, my-
self again and lonely,
even if I could?

DOMINIC HALE

Song of the Midges

> Midges as a group include many kinds of small flies; found (seasonally
> or otherwise) on practically every land area outside permanently arid
> deserts and the frigid zones.
>
> http://en.wikipedia.org/wiki/Midge

SING SING midges
to the trees the lovely trees
as we scram tarnwards in a Vauxhall Astra

and the night inflates its mussel-black
screensaver :) each star is trussed in place
those studs of ash

SING SING midges
you whirring scrawls
tarn-swilled pellets protesting
to the shady boughs :)

the #statues in the #square were blank
their faces had been scrubbed out/
deleted/photoshopped so nobody
could tell what they had looked like
this was our work

SING SING midges
in the custody of mist
you are small :) you are fat with secrets
exhumed out of the algae ditch

[At 1pm the Dr of Midgology was giving a lecture
in a locked room to an audience of midges
they did not like being told
what they were about]

recall the streets complete with cars and wind
and midges
recall the streets of midges on their phones
recall the streets of altered monuments
the #statues without faces

SING SING midges
moving over silence, you are not dead
you are dead
you are the stuff of monuments
the living shrapnel

the #statues in the #square have all been spoilt
it was the midges :)
with their buckets of froth and aerosols
they drench the wood in their graffiti:)

SING SING midges
from throats swollen with blood cells
those vortices

we are driving through your rainy wood
a man on the radio is talking about
unrest/prog rock/cardiac dysrhythmia
he is certainly a terrorist :)

they were protesting about something pointless
they were texting each other pointlessly
the city #square was all disfigured
and it is pointless

♦🖐☠♪ ♦🖐☠♪ ○♓♎♑♏♏•
SING   SING   midges
do not throw down your placards and bricks
'r u goin 2 trip0li 4 summr???'
                              ':) no sry xox'
SENDING ERROR MESSAGE NOT SENT

the #statues were worth so much now they
are worth nothing and the midges
will be blamed for such a desecration
but it was our work it was not their work
it was our work

SING SING midges
though the woods are full of powder
hosed with solvents
a fumigated nook
sing though your wings are failing
on the darkness of the tarn :)

Twice winner of the Foyle Young Poets of the Year Award – in 2009 and
2010 – Dominic Hale returned to Ledbury to give a solo reading in 2014.

SOPHIE HANNAH

My Candle
(after Edna St Vincent Millay)

My candle burns at both ends.
I cannot put it down.
I'm asking for my money back
next time I go to town.

TONY HARRISON

Black Sea Aphrodite

Chersonesos, Crimea. Archaeologists reassemble
miscellaneous pebbles to restore Aphrodite
found on the Black Sea the year of my birth,
1937, by Kiev's Prof. Belov.
An Aphrodite of pebbles made fatal as missiles
when flung by fervid adultress-denouncers,
in sects so hyper-pious they damn all such couplings,
and stipulate suitable sizes for stoning
so adultresses the goddess had goaded to lust
suffer death dragged out slowly (as they deserve!)
and not sooner snuffing with stones more grenade-size,
like those the Taurians lobbed at Orestes,
damaged child like his sister from Trojan War fallout,
as he foamed at the mouth with Furies inside him
driving him to the temple whose ruins stood here,
and Artemis made his sister priestess of.
The temple stood here where these pebbles abound,
before its marble helped make Sebastopol solid
till Crimean War then World War bombarded it flat.

The Black Sea here, between Russia and us,
part 'grating roar' part 'turbid ebb and flow'
but of Bosporus motion and not Dover Beach,
casts unmosaically onto the shore
apple-size, apricot, sugared-almond-size pebbles
and keeps casting and causing reducing abrasions,
too rounded for ducks-and-drakes but do nicely
for umbilicus, hip, pubis, little brown nipples
of the Aphrodite we gazed on not fully assembled.
I ducks-and-drakes some across the Black Sea,
my aiming eye dazzled by afternoon light shafts
that bounce off the harbours on the Russian horizon.
If my skimmed stones could only continue their skipping
they'd cover Georgia, the Caspian, Afghanistan...

I should just let them be, pushed, swooshed, re-immersed
and abraded to the size of pertish brown nipples
like these the half-doffed yellow mantle's revealing
on the Aphrodite assembled from Black Sea shore scree,
scree full of goddesses for any sized sanctum,
scooped random handfuls of shapeable shingle.

We bathe in the Black Sea then hold hands and run,
surfing so much foam-born pebble potential,
devotees of the goddess defying the stoners.

GRAHAM HARTILL

Poem for Rob

It was commonly thought that Rob couldn't really handle language,
express himself.
He wrote: *Only you can hear the glasses of teeth?*
Only you
can see behind the eyes of the movements,

you can see
the blinded pictures of the dead.
He'd hardly been to school, been in and out of care,
then worked on the coal lorries;
sat at the edge of the room, shaven,
or sometimes not, not saying much,
till he got the bug, the writing thing.
He wrote
about himself of course – apparently –
Countries
and mazes dismays and tunes, wishes to flight
in the blinded seas of their dreams
winding through from where you are, and you can see behind
their eyes, and when you fall you hear their dreams
through the graveyard, the winds
folded
through the trees...
He was getting nervous, his parole was coming up
he was pissing people off;
some said he was getting aggressive but I found that hard to
        believe.
One day, after years of talking,
he started to tell me about his family –
complicated.
He wrote:
I WISH I HEARD YOUR FIRST CRY... I WISH YOUR EYES
WOULD OPEN IN A CUPBOARD SMALL AND BARE.
Do you see from where you are?
Come to a bad end. What you never
done is gone to sleep in a bed
in the house of dreams.
The haunted gap in your mind.
I would rewrite his poems in a way that he sometimes thought
        was good,
this free-verse thing he was starting to play with, without
        understanding yet
how the precision of what we put on the page
is a rhythm, an attempt at accuracy of thought –
but then the way he thought was different from mine.

He wrote:
Through the
window you see no stars, sitting in a chair with the
quilt and looking out of the window and then
slowly your eyes stopped looking.
I would pick out certain words and passages
like this, to an end of poetry –
an effectiveness of words as they are to me,
but in fairness I give them back to him
knowing that what he gets will not be quite
what I give him
though I honour his play and his power,
language,
when he writes like this:
ONLY THEN WE REALISED OUR PLEASURE
OF FLYING THIS RED KITE.
WE STOPPED AND LOOKED, SURE WE COULD FEEL THE
*   PULL OF THE WIND.*
DARKNESS CHILLS THE STRING OUT TO ITS LIMIT
AMIDST THE CLOUDS OF A CRIMSON SKY

MATT HARVEY

In Praise of Amateur Astronomers

and some are called to watch the stars
to stay up late and scan the skies
on moonless nights with fleece and flask
to train self-educated eyes
with night-adjusted irises

they know what an aurora is
and how to plot each bright dot's orbit
participate in heaven's audit

perched on tripods pointing skyward
super strength zoom lenses lend
affordable home-hubble views
and they peruse
Io, Ganymede, the Jovian moons

the rings of Saturn, Venus' phases
they rest techno-augmented gazes
on their distant perfect curves

austere voyeurs

while here on earth
the pinpoint pricks of light observed
are living rooms with flickering screens

sat soft and vaguely comatose
before the soaps and talent shows
settee-bound households who reserve

the accolade of oohs and ahs
for different kinds of flickering stars
and viewing opportunities

a quiet step away from these
in voluntary darkness
with the patience of the ancients
in their small suburban fastness

anonymous astronomers
keep vigil with the vastness
and gaze through see-through skies
at free view stars

ROBERT HASS

■ USA

An Argument about Poetics Imagined at Squaw Valley after a Night Walk under the Mountain

My friend Czesław Miłosz disapproved of surrealism.
Not hard to construct, in imagination, the reasons why.
Late night and late winter in Warsaw: two friends
Are stopped by the police of the General Government
Who speak atrocious Polish. Because of their leather jackets –
Where would two young Poles get new brown leather jackets
In the winter of 1943? Either they were black marketeers,
The cops reasoned, or special enough to be left alone.
The older cop who had been a policeman in Berlin
In the quiet precincts of Charlottenburg where he had learned
To go along and get along and who wanted now
Only to do his job well enough to avoid being sent
To the Russian front, where he'll either be blown up
Or lose his toes to frostbite, wants nothing of this pinch.
He's the one who lets the poet slip away.
The other, younger, a machinist in Cologne before the war,
Is more ambitious. He asks the second man what he does.
Which for the young Pole is a quandary. Does he say
He is a philosopher, which is what he thinks of as his profession,
Or a teamster, which is how he makes his living now
To avoid collaborating with the Germans? And secondly
Should he answer him in Polish or in his perfect German.
He is completing, after work, in his drafty garret room
A treatise on the Apollonian and Dionysiac personalities
Described by Friedrich Nietzsche from a partly Marxist,
Partly kabbalistic perspective. He feels instinctively
That the danger lay in claiming a superior social status
And so he says in Polish that he is a teamster, and the cop
Thinks – aha! black market – and takes him in.
He's interrogated, turned over to the SS, beaten,
Interrogated some more, identified as a communist
And an intellectual and sent east to Auschwitz
Where he eventually dies, shot, some of the stories say,

Wasted by typhus and diarrhea, say the others.
The poet hears one of these versions of the news
On the same spring day that he is contemplating
A large, polished porcelain giraffe bobbing up and down
To the strains of the Vienna Waltz on a holiday carousel
While gunfire crackles on the other side of the ghetto wall.
Warsaw had been a Russian garrison town for a century.
Now it's a German garrison town and the pretty Polish girl
On the giraffe is licking a pink cloud of cotton candy
And flirting with the German officer on the zebra,
Which is also bobbing up and down, and the sheen
On his high black boots, the poet notices involuntarily,
Has picked up the reflection of the sun in the small pools
Of spring rain on the warped tarmac apron of the carousel.
After that he doesn't want to read about French poets
Walking lobsters on a leash and doesn't want to seem
To celebrate the fact that the world makes no sense.
This is how, anyway, I imagine the state of mind
Produced by the fragments of the stories he would tell me.
And here inference and anecdote give way to argument.
I would quote André Breton to him in the English translation.
'My wife with the armpits of nettletrap and St John's Eve.'
And he would say, or, anyway, now, in my imagination,
He would say, 'Well, yes, of course, I assent to armpits.
And metaphors, at which Breton excelled, just as Modigliani
Excelled at armpits. Who does not love metaphor? Its quickness
That gives us the world to taste with our common senses.
I'll tell you what terrifies me: it is the idea that 'this is like that
Is like this is like that' could be all of the story, endlessly
Repeated, the poor human imagination having evolved this
Brilliant swiftness of perception and then been stuck there,
Like a hamster in a cage, groping in the endless turnstiles
Of resemblance. We are to celebrate this? as a final conquest
Of absurdity by absurdity? The armpits of those women in Modigliani,
On the contrary, are the hollows of their arms – like this, perhaps,
Or like that, but finally this woman exposing to us this tender nest
Or dark sweetness of a wet-duck's-feather tuft of hair
In a gesture, notice, that lifts the breast slightly, indolently,
And lifts the rosy nipple and offers it to us, one of the gifts –
Also sunrise, the scent of linen, of the air before first snow –

That the world has to give poor mortals among the terrors
And confusions of being what we are.' 'Well,'
I might have said, 'if you permit me to get technical,
Modigliani is making a generalised representation
Of the idea of a particular woman.' And he: 'Exactly.
A particular being. General because being this and not that,
This not like that, this one mortal thing, is what mortality
Has given us in common.' 'And that is the Miłoszian religion?'
'Yes,' he laughs. 'In my religion, if we are going to starve,
We will starve on the pears of Cézanne and the apples of Chardin.'
He squints a little. 'In my religion metaphor makes us ache
Because things are, and are what they are, and perish.
Let us not neglect to consider the slow withering
Of the pale skin of that girl and her nest of lymph nodes
And the pheromones of love and fear. And we mustn't fail
To mention lymphatic cancers, nature's brutally stupid way
Of clearing the earth for organisms freed, temporarily,
From withering and disease and the misfiring of that avidity
To reproduce which is the special trick of the cells we were made of
In some chemical slime. And, on the subject of armpits, let us not
Neglect the distinctive smell of fear, which reminds us
That in Mr Darwin's horrific scheme we are to find beautiful
The fact that, among the higher mammals, the sauce
That gives spice to their meat is the adrenalin of pure terror,
Or worse, the adrenalin of the chase and then of terror,
And, for all we know, of despair, in the prey they are devouring.
Nature is, after all, chemistry and chemistry is this
Becomes that becomes this becomes that endlessly
Through endless witherings, endless contortions
Of mammal and reptile and insect suffering and fear.
What does it know of this armpit? That breast? Those lips
Turned to the mirror for a glistening and reddening
And the way she, a girl who did not feel pretty as a girl,
Examines her plucked, arched, perfectly elegant eyebrow
And pats lightly the slick set of her hair, a 1910s set,
That decade's set, no other's, of her thick auburn hair?'
'Do you know who she was?' I asked, suddenly curious.
'Well there were two women. Jeanne Hebuterne
Who killed herself – threw herself out a window –
She was pregnant with his child – the year after he died.

She was French. Our odalisque of the raised arms
Was Lunia Czechowska. Modigliani's dealer Zborowski
Was a poet, a minor one, and he introduced Lunia
To the painter. Zborowski was a friend of my uncle.
But he died the year I arrived in Paris that first time,
So I never met him, though I did met Czechowska.'
'You met Czechowska?' 'She had me to tea.
I was twenty-one. She must have been about forty.
Thick in the waist, and looked it. It was winter
And she wore tweed. She tested me by conducting
Our interviews – mostly about my uncle's poetry
And Zborowski's – entirely in French. I remember
Thinking that her hands looked old, early arthritis
Perhaps, and were somehow beautiful, something
Delicate in the way she served the little Noel cakes
And the tea, which I devoured. I was living
On my student's stipend and then felt humiliated
That I'd cleared the plate before she'd touched it.'
He laughed. 'And I remember her scent. Amaryllis.
The apartment near the bookstore on Rue Dupuytren
Smelled of the ginger in the cakes and black tea
And her scent of amaryllis like dry summer grass.'
Czesław was buried in a crypt – in the Krakovian church
Of St Peter of the Rock – among other Polish notables.
I hated the idea of it and still do, that his particular body
Is lying there in a cellar of cold marble and old bones
Under the weight of two thousand years of the Catholic Church.
(Thinking about this still years later, imagining this dialogue
In the Sierra dark under the shadowy mass of the mountain
And the glittering stars). Not liking the fact that it is,
Perhaps, what he would have wanted. You should
Have been buried – I'm still talking to him – on a grassy hillside
Open to the sun (the Lithuanian sun the peasants
Carved on crosses in the churchyard in your childhood)
And what you called in one poem 'the frail lights of birches.'
And he might have said no. He might have said,
I choose marble and the Catholic Church because
They say no, to natural beauty that lures us and kills us.
I say no until poor Modigliani and Zborowski
And Czechowska, the girl of the raised arms and breast,

And the grown woman with her ginger cakes
And already liver-spotted hands, and Jeanne Hebuterne
And her unborn child, have risen from the dead.'
And I say, There are other ways of thinking about this.
You described headlights sweeping a field
On a summer night, do you remember? I can quote to you
The lines. You said you could sense the heartbeat
Of the living and the dead. It was a night in July, he said,
In Pennsylvania – to me then an almost inconceivably romantic name –
And the air was humid and smelled of wet earth after rain.
I remember the night very well. Those lines not so much.

JOHN HEGLEY

A Villanelle for Mademoiselle

> The baroque composer Jean-Philippe Rameau woos the younger
> Marie-Louise Mangot (with whom he will have four children and
> be with, for the rest of his days). At the time wooing, he is at odds
> with The Encyclopedistes: Diderot, and Rousseau, more so.

Mademoiselle, this villanelle's for you.
You've set my Eighteenth Century alight.
This Love is inconvenient, but true.

The Encyclopédistes haven't got a clue;
You don't appear in anything they write.
Mademoiselle, this villanelle's for you.

This composer's ill-composed, when next to you;
My chest as though my vest is very tight.
This Love is inconvenient, but true.

A cliché, but my head is all askew.
My greatest fear, you'll disappear from sight.
Mademoiselle, this villanelle's for you.

To have you wed to me would be a coup
And I believe this revolution's right.
This Love is inconvenient, but true.

You're sweeter than the pastries that I chew.
I'm twice your age, but closer though in height.
Mademoiselle, this villanelle's for you,
This Love is inconvenient, but true.

PAUL HENRY

The White-leaved Oak

Have we not longed for a simpler love
where silence lays its infinite fields
around what is left unsaid,
where the bells in the branches are enough?

We touch fingers, to pen cumuli.
The oak has known us for centuries.
We lie down in its shade, kiss and die,
kiss and die...

■ Along with Poetry on Loan and Herefordshire Libraries, Ledbury Poetry
Festival came up with the idea of a county poet in residence in 2014. As its
first incumbent, I suggested an on-line "poetry orchard", where the nomen-
clature of Herefordshire's pomology would create a kind of apple society, à la
Edgar Lee Masters' *Spoon River Anthology* – poems, by local people, written in
the voices of Kingston Black, Cherry Permain, Handsome Norman et al.

Its culmination was a contributors' reading, devised by Chloe Garner and
held in the gardens of Hellens, the manor house in Much Marcle. The clouds
held their bladders and the year's simulated orchard became real – real trees
(draped with apple names on bright banners) and, made flesh, the cider-fuelled
voices of Stoke Edith, Eggleton Styre, Cwmmy Crab, Wormsley Pippin... A
heady day. Oh yes, and three of the audience fell off their bench, painlessly.
[PH]

SELIMA HILL

Owls

Is it only me that isn't normal?
Or could it be that everybody else

is thinking they're not so-called normal too?
Are we being dreamt in some way?
Are we being dreamt by a dreamer
who can't or won't console or even contact us;

who dreams of what she dreams must be a watchtower
where women stand with gonks and watch for owls?

BRENDA HILLMAN   ■ USA

The Bride Tree Can't Be Read

The bride tree puts down its roots
below the phyla. It is there
when we die & when we are born,
middle & upper branches reaching
the planet heart by the billions
during a revolution we don't see.

Quarks & leptons are cooling
on their infant stems, spinning the spinning
brain of matter, fled to electrical dark
water, species with names the tree
can hold in the shale shade brought
by the ambulance of art;

no one but you knows what occurred
in the dress you wore in the dream
of atonement, the displaced tree in
the dream you wore, a suffering endurable
only once, edges that sought release
from envy to a more endurable loss,

a form to be walked past, that has
outworn the shame of time,
its colors sprung through description
above a blaze of rhizomes spreading
in an arable mat that mostly
isn't simple but is calm & free –

■ Notes on Ledbury (from my journal 7/2014)

—magical carved names, in the graveyard
—shops in Ledbury, pretty & precise with poems in windows
—Neil's war anthology reading 78 million dead poetry so fragile in relation
'Louse Hunting' Isaac Rosenberg
'The dust upon the paper eye' Keith Douglas
—the British can retire at 50
—Village very quiet – will they like the activist spirit?
—the idea of the ancient woods where we walked… a nightingale? We
weren't sure… the word 'verdant'… (did you bother letting them know?)
—Bob said, 'and by supplication build a bridge to it'
—wonderful Dora Wordsworth lecture
—death as an active process
—Samina Negroche & Zoë Skoulding – performance electronica +
avantgarde – very impressive 'you enter silence at 180 degrees'
—Dog Hill Wood—natural woodlands—Silurian world 420 million years—
original woods that once covered England
blue bells, primrose, anemone, wild cherry, dog's mercury, laurel, lichen
(Xanthoroia parietina?)
—some being tormented by physical & psychological discomfort
—mostly doves, magpies, blackbirds of course
—thrilling to hear a guy reading middle English in Veronica Forrest-
Thomson's poem in my class
—Seratone 5HTP from the Apothecary! Helped me sleep
—as if the thing you could defeat were yellow & the (start of a poem)
—the doves sounding especially owl-like
—Joey Connolly's poetry ++
—the spirits miss God

—Haiku during Bob's haiku lecture
spider in my hair
during his haiku lecture
wanders off alone
—Anne Michaels: 'we are in the middle of a story no matter how close to
the precipice we are'
—between the oak & the yew, in the ancient wood, saying, give my friend
more years, give her healthy breath, give her years [BH]

JANE HIRSHFIELD ■ USA

You Go to Sleep in One Room and Wake in Another

You go to sleep in one room and wake in another.
You go to sleep in one time and wake in another.

Men land on the moon! –
Viewed in blurred black and white, in static,
on a big screen in Central Park, standing in darkness with others.

Your grandfather did not see this.
Your grandchildren will not see this.
Soon now, fifty years back.

Unemphatic, the wheelbarrowed stars hung above.

Many days, like a nephew,
resemble the one beforehand,
but they are not the one beforehand.
Each was singular, spendable, eaten with pepper and salt.

You go to sleep in one person's bed and wake in another's,
your face after toweling changed from the face that was washed.

You who were not your life nor were stranger to it,
you who were not

your name, your ribs, your skin,
will go as a suitcase that takes inside it the room –

Only after you know this can you know this.
As a knocked glass that loses what has been spilled, you will know
    this.

■ Ledbury Poetry Festival feels to me a truly communal gathering, supported
as it seems by the whole town, by the history of past writers who have lived
there, by those who come to listen so warmly and fully. Even the tilting build-
ings seemed to me to lean in to listen to the conversations passing between
them. From my generous hosts (who introduced me to a lasting hunger for
samphire), to my fellow poets, both local and from afar, the few days I spent
there enlarge themselves in retrospective affection. Kay Ryan and I both still
have the small blue ceramic dishes we were given. I bring mine out often, when
I have her to supper.   [JH]

MATTHEW HOLLIS

Causeway

Beneath the rain-shadow and washed farmhouses,
in the service of the old shore,

we waited for the rising of the road –
the south lane laden in sand,

the north in residue and wrack;
the tide drawing off the asphalt

leaving our tyres little to disperse;
still, the water under wheel was forceful –

cleft between the chassis and the sea –
that clean division that the heart rages for.

But half way out the destination
ceases to be the prize,

and what matters is the sudden breadth of vision:
to the north, a hovering headland,

to the south, a shoal of light;
the sea off-guarded, but hunting.

Between mainland and island, in neither sway,
a nodding of the needle as the compass takes its weigh.

LIU HONGBIN

Voice

As soon as we leave the tunnel of our birth,
even before our bodies are cleaned of blood,
we all cry out, and those sharp cries
are the first signs of our talent for speech.
Later, we escape in many directions, and our voices
are lamps of fire in the rain, which fly up
looking for their own lines of light,
as flocks of birds rush through the trees
or birdsong falls along forest paths.
That is how our voices mingle with air.
Who can forbid something so natural?

World, we must have a talk about this.
We don't need any language to do it,
Just to look at each other.
Nature's a womb not a refrigerator,
Our voices which are spacious as the sky,
must not be frozen in us or we die.

translated from the Chinese by Elaine Feinstein

ADAM HOROVITZ

Fire-voices

What is religion?
A shared dream of landscape
fenced with simple rules

by which to live a life of listening
for the quivering fire-voice of hope;
    some spark of kindness
in the desert's inward creep.

*

Does it still the hand
that wields a knife? No,
not always, but it is built to do so;

at least until some chancer learns
how easy it can be to throw
their voice into the fire.
Thereafter, watch the fences burn
and as they burn, watch
how the gentler truths they held mutate
into a cancer-rush of fright;

how people begin listening
to any siren song that panders to their fears,
in a flame that someone else has set.
New fences (ten feet tall and charged
with panic by the lightning bolt) will soon spring up
and then there's nothing left except
to be livestock in someone else's bonfire,

screamed at till you cannot wake,
until all that's left of thought
is the desire to fight.

*

What is faith? The tending
of empty places where structures
fail to find a foothold.

The act of reaching out
for a quivering fire-voice of hope;
        some spark of kindness
in the desert's inward creep.

MICHAEL HOROVITZ

For Felix Mendelssohn

What a wonderful life it must have been
if you were Felix Mendelssohn

                                – rediscovering Bach
and bringing him to wide public appreciation

– adored by protégés like Robert and Clara Schumann

– getting seasick on a whirl round the storm-tossed Hebrides
then stepping ashore and dashing off Fingal's Cave

– to be reprised at every second wedding all over the Christian world
for your *Incidental Music to A Midsummer Night's Dream*

    – how I'd love
                to have been him

– though, come to think of it
                                – if I *had* been him,
                                I'd be dead.

        ...Then again, perhaps I was
        Felix Mendelssohn

in another incarnation
closed to me

− till now.

Listening again
to his *Songs Without Words* on the radio
it strikes me

that if I am indeed
anything like
a composer

I have to
stop talking   − and get on
with the music.

SARAH HOWE   ■ CHINA / UK

On a line by Xu Lizhi

I swallowed a moon made of iron
you sang
the one who would stare from a fourth-storey sill
waiting for the brunt lick of dormitory fan

to come round again
pitched in the grimy glass
your still-young face electroplates with lunar currents
it clogs the sky

overtime dense as a dentist's drill
you are shower-capped again in the assembly line
your eyes acid-etched circuitries
where fatigue's fluorescent scrim settles like dawn

you float between
the rows ministering to never-ending components
their hands a flight of chrome
tongue soldered by thirst

you sway
could almost reach
the cartoon bulb twitching hot above your head
later in your bunk

among strangers hauled from sundry provinces
who fart like dogs in their sleep
you write down a line about the screw that fell
with an unheard plink

to the factory floor
words I read on a screen that reels at my touch
and choke
then tap the next link

Xu Lizhi was a Chinese poet and Foxconn factory worker who committed
suicide, aged 24, in 2014.

LESLEY INGRAM

Garter

Midsummer's eve:
you peel an apple

its skin a snake
a stocking ribbon

and curl it
under your pillow.

In your dreams
you see me

offering my life
and the small

stranglehold
of marriage.

In the morning
a soft, red bruise.

This poem is from The Poetry Orchard, a Ledbury Poetry Festival project in
partnership with Poetry on Loan and Herefordshire Libraries in 2014. Prompted
by Herefordshire poet in residence Paul Henry's poem 'Windfalls', writers
contributed poems based on the names of Herefordshire apples. See note on
page 119 and www. poetry-festival.co.uk/the-poetry-orchard/

HELEN IVORY

Wunderkammer with Weighing Scales and Hospital Bed
(FROM *The Anatomical Venus*)

She breaks the bread into tiny pieces
and places them on the table
that floats above her father's bed.

He is already gone but his breathed-out air
cannot help but enter her body
and claim her lungs as kin.

How selfish her hunger was;
how utterly inappropriate.

She presses the bread to parchment thinness;
holds it up to the panel of light.

SARAH JAMES

The Man Who Raced Fire

He'd never seen such a horse before:
the size of its flanks, black but
an unending tail of orange and reds.

The galloping stallion was racing his truck, jumped
bushes, fences, trees, homes…
His speedometer soared and then

he couldn't keep up with the pound of hooves
kicking up smoke, gas tanks exploding,
as stones cracked his windscreen sky.

■ Warm, welcoming, and wonderful words – Ledbury is a delight to read at and to enjoy other poets' readings. But it's also more than that; it's a week of poetry buzz, chat and inspiration. I've discovered so many unique and unusual poetry projects for the first time through Ledbury. I also particularly treasure memories of hearing international poets read, such as C.D. Wright. It is amazing to have this, and to not have to travel to London for it. [SJ]

MEIRION JORDAN

Phaedo

But when I am gone, if you meet some stranger –
from our own country –
at the gate of some dusty peninsular town
where the dogs bark in the streets at noon

and nobody knows anything of the way
we used to wear our caps, and what it meant
to us then, I want you to talk

not of the simplicity of it, how
when we die we simply lie down and wait
for the circumstances to reach our hearts,

but I want you to repeat to them things we have said together
about the immortality of the soul,
how it may be held jealously close to this life
by the body's love, or, to spare us pain
it goes quickly and it disappears.

And as you are talking with this person
not well-known to you, I want you to think of the times
when young men who were eager for me –
for the things I possessed in my mind only –
would be so brave as to roll themselves up in my cloak with me,
and we would forget about the girls with their flutes,
and the cicadas singing loud at the window.

And there are many other things I would like you to think.
Of the young men, who I loved, who I have always loved:
of how you have been a friend, and more than a friend,
to me; of my strange dreams of music. Or how
in my house even now the wine-jars
do not stand empty.

And then I want you to embrace this stranger,
this person with whom you share nothing except a homeland,
and I want that you should kiss, as good friends do, in despite of
        everything,
and then go again on your way, past the olive trees
and the shepherds who have never heard of any of us.

JENNY JOSEPH

Two Journeys

Baby George and Aged P
Bottom shuffling on the stairs
One going up, one going down

Sat in the middle, gazed with surprise
Warm fat flesh cuddles lean hard flank
Half way up and half way down

Old tweed covers clean new crawlers
Gurgles and laughing, nuzzling and kisses
Baby George and Aged P
One going up, one going down

Continued their way

DORIS KAREVA   ■ ESTONIA

from Septachord

Snow is a blank sheet.
            Underneath
ciphers glow unseen –
the trumpet solo of spring,
the saffron shade of summer.

Snow is a blank sheet.
                Do not write
there a single name;
let stars be reflected
in countless crystals.

Each flake is a star,
altogether unique
in insignificance –
    all dissolves.

Snow is a blank sheet
and solace –
    silence of language,
aquiver with meaning.

translated from the Estonian by Miriam McIlfatrick-Ksenofontov

KAPKA KASSABOVA   ■ BULGARIA / UK

It's Always Strange to Sleep in Cities

It's always strange to sleep in cities
you haven't seen in daylight.
You could be anywhere, anybody
could be breathing next door. In the night
under used blankets you dream
of waking to the highest spires,
fastest clouds, brightest snow.

You dream of drunken rooftops
strewn with broken stars
and you dream of some people you've known.
They're here in the streets,
on the rooftops, in the windows
of the city which is – you awake to find –
nothing but shadows and fog.

It seems they've always been here.
And you tell them without words
because words are not
in the nature of this dream

how happy you are to be here.
How alone, unsure
of the future, of the past.

They thank you for your visit,
everything is fine, they say,
their mouths opening without a voice,
they hope to see you again.
But they don't touch you. Then dawn
breaks over the city
where it is always strange to sleep.

JACKIE KAY

April Sunshine

When the people who have lived all of their lives,
For democracy, for democracy,
Survive to see the spring, April sunshine,
It's a blessing it's a blessing.

In the hospital this bleak mid winter,
You were just an old woman;
You were just an old man.

Nobody imagined how you marched against Polaris,
How you sat down at Dunoon – stood up for U.C.S.
Nobody pictured you writing to Mandela
And fifty other prisoners of South Africa.

In the hospital this bleak mid winter,
You were just an old woman;
You were just an old man.

Nobody knew you greeted Madame Allende
Or sang the songs of Victor Jara

Or loved Big Arthur's bravura Bandiera Rossa
Or heard Paul Robeson at the May Day rally

You were just an old woman;
You were just an old man.

Nobody knew you saw all of 7:84
The Steamie and *Bevellers* opening nights...
How you cried with laughter!
How you stood up for the Arts.

How you stood up for the Arts!

In the hospital, throughout this long winter, you were just an old
        woman;
You were just an old man.

How you went to concerts every Friday at RSAMD
And how just last Saturday you were mad
You couldn't march against Trident with Nicola Sturgeon.

You say: *One less missile would subsidise the arts for a century!*
You say: *Which politician will stand up for the arts!*

You would have struggled with your new grey stick!
You would have walked with your poppy red zimmer.
To march against Trident once more,
To march against Trident stridently!

What do we want? You say! *Peace in society.*
Time has not made your politics dimmer.

When the people who lived all of their lives
For democracy, for democracy,
Survive to see the springtime, April sunshine,
It's a blessing it's a blessing.

■ I love Ledbury, one of my favourite festivals anywhere. Its hospitality and
spirit is memorable, and each visit there has given me quite a lift. My parents
came twice with me and just loved Ledbury, the big suppers in the tilting hall,
the massive pork pies, the sofas on the street, the spark and buzz of the most
hospitable of festivals surround by the beautiful Malvern Hills... [JK]

LUKE KENNARD

Balcony

Listen: as a child I thought of being a soldier
in the Devil's army, vanquished in the last battle,
ceasing to exist, and nothing forever.

An angel killed me and then there was nothing.
No dark or light element to silently float in,
no element; no floating; no subject or object:
no soft barometer to register the nothing.
no critics of the neither abject nor beautiful nothing.

Like fastening a necklace you aren't wearing;
trying to soothe a looped recording of a crying baby;
Like lighting a fire with the wood you chopped in a game.

But if I concentrated, I could feel it,
before I knew the words *infinity* or *oblivion*:

It does not end or begin: there is no outside of it, or if there is
that is where we are now briefly perched:
we play with toy cars or lounge smoking on a very

privileged loggia. And then I thought:
I am lucky to have put away such unforgiving fantasies,
but then I thought now for a certainty this is the only balcony.

■ I remember reading at Ledbury after being shortlisted for the Forward Prize in 2007, and I remember the Forward shortlisting being something of a mixed blessing; it meant more people read my poems and that they were more likely to resent me. I remember the Ledbury audience sitting in Penguin deck chairs and I remember waiting before the reading in a building on stilts. I remember being a little star-struck by other writers. I remember completely unlit pub gardens and, for some reason, drinking beer out of a bowl. I remember being very hungover and eating a very good Scotch egg. I have no recollection of the poems I read, but a vague sense that the audience were generous and my hosts extremely hospitable. [LK]

AMY KEY

An Abecedary of Unrequited Love

unrequited love for auto-connecting to your wifi
unrequited love for being looked at with faux-disapproval
for cornichons, derelict swimming pools, extreme pallor
unrequited love for first name / last name symmetry
unrequited love for girls curling their eyelashes on the top deck
his strange weather – imaginary boyfriends – junk food's made a comeback
unrequited love for kirby grips, Lee Miller's selfies, my own metanarrative
unrequited love for no fixed ideal
for optic measures
for paint tester pots
for queenliness
unrequited love for ring-pull cans – sexually aggressive mixtape song
      choices – teen talk
unexpected cover versions
Valley Girls
unrequited love for waving at wrist-height to someone standing next to
      you / 'wear your clothes, pretend I was you, and lose control' /
      'wear your pink glove all the time' / water slides / when someone
      on a bicycle bumps into a friend on a bicycle and they try to hug
      without getting off their bicycles
unrequited love for xylophones
unrequited love for your salvage yard eyes
unrequited love for Zelda Fitzgerald, who died in a fire while awaiting
      electroshock therapy. Nine women, including Zelda, died that day.

■ I first read at Ledbury in 2013 in a poetry show at Hellens Manor produced by Jaybird Live Literature. I imagined how wonderful it would be to live in that magical place. Then, last year, I returned to Hellens to take part in a Ledbury-sponsored voice coaching workshop, and stayed for four days on the estate. It was a very special few days of making friends and facing some fears. We were sent off into the gardens to memorise our poems in preparation for a performance later that day. Whispering my own poems to myself as I wandered around the wildflower meadow at Hellens will always stay with me. [AK]

MIMI KHALVATI ■ IRAN / UK

Glose: The Summer of Love, 1967

> But even in the summers we remember
> The forest had its eyes, the sea its voices,
> And there were roads no map would ever master,
> Lost roads and moonless nights and ancient voices...
>
> DONALD JUSTICE, 'Sadness'

That was the year in Shawshank Prison that Red
was paroled and hitched a ride to Zihuatanejo,
little place on the Pacific. As Andy said,
'a warm place with no memory' to go to
after the battles, burials – JFK buried
at Arlington, the Six-Day War, Biafra
born only to die an infant death – with no
family, home, no baggage. So there they fled –
two men with a past in that long hot summer.
But even in the summers we remember

– and who'd forget the summer of love, the rallies,
Be-Ins, fighting for peace armed with guitars,
the Sioux, South Dakota in facepaint with hippies
wearing bedsheets, carnations, paper stars
and us in black leotards for our first sally
onstage swanning around in star-struck poses,
Ruth so fond, Rory foolish, Tusse, Barra,
like a sun, a moon, Julian who died and Jimmy? –
yes, even in those days of wine and roses,
the forest had its eyes, the sea its voices.

Little did I dream when we did our audition
I'd marry Paul one day and have his kids.
While *Puppet on a String* won Eurovision,
the Shah was crowned, Elvis himself got married,
I was dreaming, as Andy was, of redemption,
of 'an entirely novel kind of star', a pulsar,
nebula, lightmap of some bright beloved.

138

Bright? Just as stars spun out of all proportion,
black holes were named, the Milky Way grew vaster
and there were roads no map would ever master.

Some of us fell from grace, others found fame,
fortune or sank quietly out of sight,
seen only by the forest. Back in Chalk Farm,
our rehearsal rooms, black-ceilinged, -floored, daylight
still flanked by blackout shutters and the same
backstairs, church portico, return bays, arches,
breathe through the dark thicket. I could take fright –
to end up here so lonely. That's why I came.
That's where I found you, friends, as age approaches,
lost roads and moonless nights and ancient voices.

JOHN KINSELLA   ■ AUSTRALIA / UK

Playing Cricket at Wheatlands

An on-drive to the boundary the ball
going on and on through dust and dirt
on and on past the shed all the way past
the chook pen and on bouncing over
bark flaked and fallen from wandoos
and on over dried twigs and branches
and chunks of quartz – rose, milky –
on and on under the loosely strung fence
on and on over the dry ploughed ground
of the 'new' pig yard on and on uphill
gathering speed against gravity perpetual
motion itself on and on over firebreaks
past pig melons the only green hugging
the ground in mid autumn still hot
and the blond sheen of old stubble
though behind the wicket some deeply

ploughed paddocks where brief rain
inspired prematurely and beyond
them the mysterious Needlings Hills
with granites and roos and markings
telling stories of country deeper
than survey pegs but back to the ball
which rolls on and on right over
contour banks at a tangent to the house-
dam with its velvet-rippled-baked-
mud walls and murky shallow eye
courtesy of those brief rains and on
up into the Top Bush where nest-robbers
inspired anger and bewilderment and
a children's story starring all of us –
especially my cousin Ian (wicket-keeping)
and cousin Ken (first slip) caught ready
to take the catch when I surprised them all
by driving the ball a bit on the up but still
on and on past the demon bowler
who was probably my brother Stephen
or my uncle Gerry – on and on scattering
a flock of pink & greys scrounging
for seed on and on past a pair of crows
eyeing off the body parts of small creatures
we can't or won't see and on and on
into the distant purple mountain
and through the setting sun and on
into night that will fall over all
our games fall on and beyond
the farm our field of play.

KO UN

Little monk Ilyeon's journey

(FROM *Maninbo, volume 27*)

Engulfed in a blizzard, still fearless.
Not an inch
could he see ahead of him.
Aged fifteen
the novice monk Ilyeon, who had received the Ten Precepts.
was moving that day
of all days
to another temple,
engulfed in a blizzard.

No going forward, no going back, all alone.
What to do?
What to do?

One branch of an ancient pine stretched out, covered in snow.
He set out blindly
in the direction that branch was stretching.
Went blindly in the direction that branch
was pointing.
Ploughing through snowdrifts, falling into the snow
he went on and on.
After he had walked for more than half a day
it grew dark.
What to do?
What to do?

Just then
a gleam of light appeared as if in a dream.
The direction shown by the pine branch had been correct.

A phrase he had learned somewhere burst from little Ilyeon's lips:

From this day on
take the sad sound of birdsong
as your true friend.

translated from the Korean by Brother Anthony of Taizé & Lee Sang-Wha.

■ By the time I and Ko Un with his wife had flown from Korea and arrived in Ledbury on July 9, most of the festival's events were over. Alas! Realising belatedly how much we had missed, we wished we had set off much earlier. But that was compensated for by the wonderful privilege of spending the last days of the festival as Adam Munthe's guests at Hellens. For us, that meant that the festival became a joyful family gathering, with long hours spent in convivial exchanges during leisurely meals in lovely surroundings. The festival events that we could enjoy only told us much more clearly that we should have come earlier, attended more, and met the poets who had already left by the time we arrived. Ah well, if ever another Korean poet has the good fortune to be invited… I know what advice I must give as to the date of our arrival! [BAoT]

NICK LAIRD

The Good Son

I

The deconstructionist in us might gloss
that last request as *Bring back my phallus.*

I'm thinking how even after Hamlet senior
stage-whispers *Adieu!* to his son, his heir –
his piglet and little poppet, his lovely –
how he begs him again *Remember me,*

since he can't help himself, and the actor
says it back and swears it on his honour,
and by convention is meant there and then
to whip out his sword and avenge, avenge –

but sits down instead, shrugs off his mantle
to undo his satchel and pulls out a quill
and a clean pad to get it in detail –

which the Elizabethans deem a scandal.

II

We did. We paid upfront but understood
that all accounts would soon be met
and every tab discharged in full.

Each loss incurred a debt
and hard to get the registers to balance.

This side of Cookstown Gospel Hall attests
in giant gothic font –
For the Wages of Sin is Death…

then a few yards round the corner,
nailed up in Monrush to a telephone pole,
an unfaded statement in fairly crude
red, white and blue on plywood –

Murder in Texas gets the electric chair.
In Magherafelt you get chair of the council.

III

The rigour functioning in Sophocles
as justice we cannot retrofit with peace:
an animal language inadequate
to state the state of the state.

Hard to think some companies
were simply unafraid to leave
aside the long soliloquy:

natural, simple, affecting

Garrick had the whole fifth act rewritten
so when Claudius orders Hamlet to get
immediate to England, his reaction
is to draw his blade, and let him have it.

I mean that Hamlet stabs him.

VALERIE LAWS

Lobotomy I: Walter Jackson Freeman II
(Inventor of the Transorbital Lobotomy in 1946)

Breakthrough? A medical miracle! My method takes minutes
To cure schizoprenia – splits emotion from intellect, cuts
Thalamo-cortical connections of prefrontal cortex
And – but hey, forget jargon. I'm a scientist, trust me, this,
This is simple. My first leucotome? An icepick from the kitchen!
No need to be scared. I just drive this spike deep into the brain,
Skimming each eyeball, right through the socket. Hammer
It home, crack the orbital bone. Swing the pick like
A pendulum, hammer again, give one expert wrench,
Simple and safe, bam! Fixed. Anyplace is my theatre,
No need for a surgeon; no messing, no fuss,
No dressings, no gloves. Watch me do left and right, both
Eyes at once – twenty-five lucky gals in one day, yes sir!
Desperate mania, suicidal ravings, I'll wipe out
Any shameful cravings. Change your wife's personality,
Cure stepson's sulks, Mom's migraines. Communism.
Electroshocks knock 'em out, humane and so cheap,
Two hundred dollars buys a biddable wife, daughter, son,
No more mania, not sleeping, no moping or weeping. Safe?
I've done thousands! Rosemary Kennedy got a bit lippy,
Went a bit wild, worried her Pa, so we put her straight.
Now she lives with the nuns guaranteed safe from scandal,
An innocent soul. Good as gold, a real doll.

So go on. Have yours done. Sign here, so. Watch me go.

This is the first of a sequence on lobotomy inspired by photographs by John Hirsch of his grandmother Lurine whom he discovered had been subjected to the procedure.

GWYNETH LEWIS

Ornithology

The Wood Thrush sings a duet
All by itself, using two separate
Voices, while the whip-bird's one cry – two creatures,
Nothing between them, though you know the fiction,
Standing on Point Sublime, to listen:
'One. Are we one. We are. One.'

LIZ LOCHHEAD

Persimmons
(for Tom)

you must've
loved
those three globes of gorgeous orange
dense and glowing in our winter kitchen
enough
to put coloured-pencil and biro to the
reddest page left in your rainbow sketchbook
and make this drawing of
three persimmons in that Chinese bowl.

the supermarket flagged them up as
this season's sharon fruit
but we prefer persimmon (for
didn't it seem the rose of
their other name
would neither taste or sound as sweet,
would be a fruit of quite
another colour?)

such strange fruit... we bit and ate,
enjoyed.
before we did you drew them.
– oh you'd say so what
(drawing, to you, is as everyday as apples)
but I know
they'd have come and gone like Christmas
if you'd not put them down
and made them worth more than the paper
they're inscribed on – see
those deft strokes of
aquamarine and white that
make our table-top lie flat, the fruits
plump out real and round and
perfectly persimmon-coloured
upon their lilac shadows in the bowl's deep-
still life
still life, sweetheart,
in what's already eaten and done with.

now, looking, I can taste again.

MICHAEL LONGLEY

The Snowdrops

Inauspicious between headstones
On Angel Hill, wintry love
Tokens for Murdo, Alistair,
Duncan, home from the trenches,
Back in Balmacara and Kyle,
Cameronians, Gordon Highlanders
Clambering on hands and knees
Up the steep path to this graveyard
The snowdrops whiten, green-
Hemmed frost piercers, buttonhole
Or posy, Candlemas bells
For soldiers who come here on leave
And rest against rusting railings
Like out-of-breath pallbearers.

DAVE LORDAN   ■ IRELAND

Tiger Blowjob

I debated a while whether to call this poem
Language or *The English Language* or *English*
or *The Entrepreneur* or *Current Pedagogic Methodology* or *School*
or even English School but it wasn't a school
in spite of its departmental stamps and certificates
and its 1200 registered clients, each handing over
thousands and thousands in fees.
It was just a second floor office
in Tiger Central above a tanning lounge
and next door to a corporate paint-balling agent's
and it was far from the only operation

that instead of selling lessons was, with greater acumen,
selling attendance. 90 ticks. 90 teacher's ticks were needed
at the end of every 6 month period
for the GNIB (Garda National Immigration Bureau)
to examine and then, finding all else satisfactory,
consent to renew those special ex-EU work-and-study
visas which gave contingent sanction to a quota
of mainly young and transient cheap-labour emigrants
to work in the western world as long as they attended
those expensive English Lessons for a mandatory five
days a week leaving little choice to each but make
the tills continually click for the bosses of
convenience stores while handing up
the bulk of their wages to the Language Schools,
and the remainder to their landlords
(I heard of teenage Chinese sleeping nine to a room)
so that they couldn't make any decent money for themselves
or to remit before working a sixty-hour week
which doesn't leave much concentration
left for learning lists of past participles
or filling in blanks in the future conditional.
It wasn't long before many students discovered,
like many since and before them, that you can learn
more English in even or especially the shittiest job
just because you have to learn it
to get by than you ever could in a school or university
and you'll earn more money too and send bigger bundles
home and it wasn't long either before some of the bosses
in the Language Schools came to realise that not-teaching
could be just as lucrative as teaching, could be
a million wad just dangling there in front of you
and all you had to do was make a grab
and so my mate, who worked for this Quality Assured
Guaranteed Irish Departmentally Certified school
one summer as its Academic Manager, whenever
a young woman from Recife or Nanjing or Mauritius
would turn up centless in a sob because the boyfriend
had pissed or mah-jonged the earnings or she had been
needle-mugged or she had wired it to buy back
her little sister from the mob or it was crocodile

or whatever and she couldn't or wouldn't pay
for the attendance ticks but had come to beseech him
like Magdalene anyway, well my mate would, decently,
let her away with it, providing absolutely every tick she needed
for the small consideration of a blowjob.

*

I debated for a while what I should call this poem
and I considered *Visadick* and *LinguaCock* and *CocKtionary*
and *The man whose lad had visas in it*
and *The man who came language* and even *Liquidity*
but none of the above had the bite
the clamp the rip the chomp the chew the suck
the roaring thirst the burning goo for blood
and piss
and spunk
and words
I think this story wanted.

HANNAH LOWE

If You Believe: Old Paradise Street

If you believe I played with Phil Seamen in 1970,
a Sunday night, The Dog and Bone half empty,
Phil just keeping time with his sticks in one hand
and then, when the punters flocked in,
his hands a blur on the ghost notes and flams,
you may as well believe anything I dream of
looking at his old album covers –
how on the bus to gigs he'd beat a Yoruba groove
on his knees, or mine, while the passengers stared,
one knee the high-hat, one the snare
or how we drank the night down in the flat
on Old Paradise Street, his record player

spinning through Ghana, through Cuba,
Phil just tapping his feet or later, a fag spilt
from his half-moon heroine grin:
Don't you know at midnight I turn into a pumpkin?
Rack-thin in his old cardigan, drooped
in his chair, but what he knew about drumming
was like opening the door to let the sunshine in.
Or you might as well believe that last try
at getting clean, stood on the Burton canal
with his fishing pole or strolling the streets
where the boy he'd been had thrown
the windows wide and whacked his drums
over the backyards and washing lines,
had nearly set him right – 'Phil's Renaissance'
Melody Maker said of the gigs we played
if you could sugar-coat the sweats and sores, the sick.
Who'd guess a nap in his chair would be
the good long sleep? Worn heart, barbiturate-weak.
Goodnight Phil. There's a bright moon tonight
on Waterloo, and the hiss of vinyl on your turntable
spinning spinning the long night through –

RODDY LUMSDEN

Objects at Rest

The comma is in placed repose. A pebble
I kicked which changed the world's balance.
A wall, being a made thing, but sitting
where it was damnedly placed. Flowers

blunt on a windless day. An empty bottle
in the binbag's sump, needless. Nothing
happening. But all the philosophers sense
the sour, drear hope of our unhappening.

150

And all too soon I'm with you, not moving,
shunted near to sleep below the duvet.
Object at Rest, ah yes, a minor painting
by Bacon or by Goya. A stripling movie

by Hitchcock. A thought I thought a marvel
which has not nailed an inch way, ever since.

ROGER McGOUGH

Aubade

Needler Hall, the University of Hull.

Woken at dawn to the sound of Bechet's clarinet
coming from his room on the floor above,
as he opens the door and creeps down the stairs.

The flop of moth-eaten brocade slippers
along the corridor. The knock. 'Come in.'
He stands in the doorway plain as a wardrobe.

'Sorry to... Unearthly hour...'
He stays just on the edge of vision,
'Thought you might be able to help.'

There is no escape. The curtain-edges grow light
and the room takes shape. 'Work has to be done.
What year was the Beatles' first LP?'

'Nineteen sixty-three,' I mumble.
'*ABBAB*. Excellent.' And he is gone.
The sky is white as clay, with no sun.

JAMIE McKENDRICK

The Hunters

We that have been hunting all the day
are mighty tired, our hair is dank with sweat
and by our hunting helmets plastered flat.

As days of hunting go, this must be counted
a good day: the horns blew loud and the dogs
barked hard as though they knew it was more for them

than us we went out hunting the wild beast
all day – so they could teach him just how tame
they were, and how wrong to think that being dogs

had taken the edge off their appetite
for sport. We that have been hunting all the day
will keep on hunting through the night

for finer creatures than the forests hide,
through forests deeper than the ones of day.

LACHLAN MACKINNON

WCW

Saxifrage, said William Carlos Williams, was his flower
because it split stone. Yesterday, in a pot, a clump of it,
weedy red petals, stems robust as peasant legs.

It would survive a summer's rage for decking,
frost memory, meltwater gush, black August.
It wouldn't last a weekend in the jungle,

being a flower of the far north, temperate at best.
Williams was a doctor, and he could listen to his language
for the slightest sign, like a stethoscope.

Saxum is stone, frag the root of *frangere*, to break.
Latin names for northern things govern them like an empire
but mean they can be passed on, spoken of

where they are not much found, like hippogriffs or cannibals
(one Greek and Latin, one misheard *Cariba*).
Williams had time for the weedy ones, men, women, children

who hang on, who pull through, saxifrage splitting stone.

ANDREW McMILLAN

last train

the threeseaters have become beds
for the last workers out of Sheffield
one young man reclines as if in
a sauna   when the heat has loosened
the body   and the balls are at their lowest
what would it be to lay with him
naked as a navvy   to lick him dry
of the day he's had   to be still with him
as the night outside hardens down to coal

IAN McMILLAN

He Finished Up Down Nine-clog Pit

He started off apprenticed
To an older man with laugh-lines
Who taught him all the right ways
And took his time explaining
Till the young man got it right

Listen to what I have to say
As Monday limps to Saturday
Or you'll finish up down Nine Clog Pit

He grew into the workplace
Ate his sarnies in the corner
And the older man grew older
And took his time explaining
In the blinding shop floor light

Listen to what I have to say
As Monday limps to Saturday
Or you'll finish up at Debney's Dump

Learning piled on learning
Till he knew the ropes and wrinkles
Ate his sarnies in the corner
Could do the job like clockwork
From the clock-on to the hooter

Listen to what I have to say
As Monday limps to Saturday
Or you'll finish up with Black-top shakes.

And then he was the old man
With no one left to talk to
To do the job like clockwork
Cos the jobs had all been outsourced
And the hours had all been zeroed

Listen to what I have to say
As Monday limps to Saturday
Or you'll finish up with broken dreams

And learning's not a lean-to
No, it can be a palace
But someone has to live there
Or knowledge ends-up homeless
Cos the jobs had all been outsourced

Listen to what I have to say
As Monday limps to Saturday
Or you'll finish up at Nine-Clog pit
Or you'll finish up in Debney's Dump
Or you'll finish up with Black-top shakes
Or you'll finish up with broken dreams

ANGUS MacNEACAIL

art, lived
(i.m. john bellany)

that he should go, with brush in hand,
engaged in dialogue with what had been
mute canvas, seems apropos, we might
have wished the breath had held its
                                    measure
longer,
        when a mind, still hungering to tell
another composition, still engaged in
shaping, shading, realising how the vital
shifting substance of an exact place
could be made new, again, again, again

a sailor of harbours who knew
all the stories of storms and
                      stupendous plimsoll-
drowning catches his own kin had told,
he believed in what he saw and drew it
out in colours fierce and joyous

he knew how to lay it on thick, to stipple,
stroke his pigment into lives and lived-in
patterns of tenement and trawler,
                              drank
deep from the well of changes, kept
his vision true, spoke to the world until
that final pause (his story cannot end

HOLLIE McNISH

Dandelions

When it all seems too much
and I wonder why we're here
and I think about the sun
and I wonder why it's there
and my daughter points to space
and the emptiness upsets me
and I lament my lack of God
and I wish that one would find me
and I worry what is out there
and I wonder what the point is
and I panic about death
and I panic it's all pointless
and I wonder when space stops
and what the fuck we're on this rock for

I think of strawberries in the summer
bright and ripe and juicy
and how perfectly dandelions seeds
are made to helicopter breezes
procreating across fields

and I remind myself
it's not all about you, Hollie

NIKOLA MADZIROV ■ MACEDONIA

The Cross of History

I dissolved in the crystals of undiscovered stones,
I live among the cities, invisible
as the air between slices of bread.
I'm contained in the rust
on the edges of the anchors.
In the whirlwind I am a child
beginning to believe in living gods.
I'm the equivalent of the migrant birds
that are always returning, never departing.
I want to exist among the continuous verbs,
in the roots that sleep
among the foundations of the first houses.
In death I want to be
a soldier of undiscovered innocence,
crucified by history
on a glass cross through which
in the distance flowers can be seen.

translated from the Macedonian by Peggy and Graham W. Reid

VALERIO MAGRELLI

Tombeau de Totò

As an old man, Totò became blind.
All that rubber-limbed gallivanting
just to end up in the dark.
A tentative groping,
a zigzag through darkness.
But the opposite is also true.
As a blind man, he became old.
I still remember him, nearby my house,
crossing the street for a funeral,
between two wings of a cheering crowd.
And he was playing along, disjointed, moving jerkily,
without seeing anything – that, I've only just understood!
Blind, old and mechanical,
but wound up by the steel spring of his Neapolitan dialect.

At least until, having lost his sight, he also lost his speech.
In his last films, unable to say his lines,
he had to be dubbed. The story goes
that having gone blind he then went dumb
in the film, while another voice had to stand in
for his own.
Blasphemous Totò-fakery, on the verge of darkness.

His vision extinguished, his speech annulled,
the ragtag body descends into the grave.

translated from the Italian by Jamie McKendrick

Totò (1898–1967), the stage name of Antonio De Curtis, was a famous Italian comedian, actor and singer.

MAITREYABANDHU

New Songs, Old Gladness

The pine trees have bent
their heads together
in a green conversation.
They have withdrawn

somewhat into themselves.
Their silence at night
is not the silence, merely,
of absent birdsong – they stand

more separately, stiller.
Having no new songs to sing,
they are not full of poems.
Their silence is deeper

than the hush of wind, simpler
than the rocks sentinel.
Walk out among them,
if you will, as among tipped

columns of darkness.
If you look up, you'll see
they hold nothing at all
except a scattering of stars.

BILL MANHIRE

20 Stanzas in the Haunted House

So the ghost appeared
and asked could he recite one of his poems.
OK, I said, feeling a little strange, just a little bit
frightened. Of course I don't actually believe in ghosts
but this one seemed legitimate and spooky. The poem
itself was a quite long poem, all about wind and water
and navigating by the stars, and he declaimed it
in an uncannily spectral manner,
so that when his words finally reached shore
I was just about asleep. I could hear lake-water lapping.
What do you think? he said. I would really
welcome your comments. To be honest, I replied,
I can't imagine any way you could begin to make that poem better.
I really liked the 22nd stanza. He turned then and cursed me,
cursed *The Paris Review*, cursed all my issue,
and slowly dissolved in the mirror.

JACK MAPANJE

Greetings from Grandpa
(for Joseph, Daniel, Nathan & Co)

You said I should write
you a teeny-weeny poem,
a poem that's easy to recite
to Alexandra and Ethan;
I am sending you a poem
that relates and leaps like
the pelican on Okavango
Delta, leaping from green

water lilies to brown floats,
a poem which springs like
the sly monkeys of Gaborone
screeching from tree branch
to rooftop, a poem which
rings bells day and night,
here, there, everywhere like
the lead–cows of The Village;
tomorrow I will send you
a wee poem which rumbles
like the lion or roars like
father–drums, a wee poem
that quivers and smokes
like the muscles of Batswana
dancers bouncing at their
brides' wedding jamboree.

GLYN MAXWELL

Photos from Before

Pity and envy now for our late selves
in photos from before, when we led lives
we have to deal with now. There was a lark
we all were in on, and we can't have back
the pronoun as it was. What was it for?
We lulled ourselves into an atmosphere.
I I escape to, where the forest trees
are green and sleepless and I realise
they're each about to turn. And how that feels
is like a wade through growing boys and girls
who think my jaw will drop. Perhaps they saw
my face in an old photo from before,
and search for any hint I have a clue
they have in mind to do what they have to do.

Reproduce!

One who does not
Rots to the core
Or is he more—
Not less—alive,
Self-possessed.
As cells divide
To multiply
Time out of mind,
The I none binds.

[*Harvard Review*, 41, Winter 2011]

Self Made

Escapes, narrow
As a hair's breadth,
Kept him in shape—
No slack, self made
Not held back.

'All escapes are narrow'

'This aphorism of mine should, might, be quoted below the poem.'
[September 3, 2009]

[July 2009: unpublished]

Repose

Fingers enfold
Hands in repose
Upon my chest—
Ahead of me
I see my toes,
Bless the bed

[March 2009: unpublished]

Awake

Round as Adam
Was before Eve—
Ribcage intact
In his old age—
He lacks nothing
He does not have
At once, awake

[November 2009: unpublished]

Time Out of Mind

1

As cells divide
To multiply
In the brain's hive
Stings, not honey
Enliven me
Time out of mind

2

Was I once
In the middle
Of my life
With half of it
Yet to come
Like a visit
Made on the run

[December 3, 2009: unpublished]

Warm in Wool

Warm in wool, not a wolf
In sheep's clothing
(Whom would I deceive
When I feel as good
As Red Riding Hood)
I praise sheep shorn
To keep me warm

[*Common Knowledge*, 11.3, Fall 2005]

NEIL ASTLEY

In Praise of Samuel Menashe

For me – and for many others – the most memorable poet to visit Ledbury was the Anglophile American, Samuel Menashe, then aged 82, giving his first and only reading in Britain for many years, in July 2008. Chairing the Saturday afternoon event – and drawing the audience for a poet most of us had been unfamiliar with – was the usually garrulous Professor Christopher Ricks, editor of a new selection of Menashe's poems, whose presence was soon rendered largely irrelevant as Menashe took over and gave an extraordinary performance which he told everyone was his 'swansong' – and sadly it turned out to be just that.

I almost missed that unmissable event. Walking down Church Lane earlier that day, I had bumped into Peter Arscott, who was showing Samuel around the town and introduced us. 'Are you coming to my reading?' he immediately demanded, and launched into a short poem. We talked more, and something touched on in our conversation summoned another poem for the occasion. It soon became evident that he knew all his poems by heart. I hadn't bought a ticket for his reading, but kept quiet about that, heading for the box office as soon as we parted.

As the Ledbury audience were to discover, Samuel Menashe's poems are all very short. The whole of life is distilled in a few lines. He recited – or said – poem after poem, linking them with anecdotes, and occasionally letting Ricks get a word in. A learned question from the professor set Samuel off on another stream of stories and poems, none of them read from the book, all said from memory and spoken so directly with full eye contact that everyone in the audience thought he was reading just to them. Ledbury loved him and Samuel basked in their admiration. Some people were in tears. The bookstall only had ten copies of the American edition and I made sure I got one of them.

Each of his poems has a mysterious simplicity, a spiritual intensity and a lingering emotional force. Like Kay Ryan's similarly short poems, each poem is packed with meaning, its wit released through quirky wordplay. They are often so short that they're over before you know it, and you have to re-read them several times for their brilliance to become fully apparent. Like Kay Ryan again, Samuel would often read or rather say his poems twice, to give you a second chance of taking them in. They are brief in form but profound in their engagement with ultimate questions. As Stephen Spender wrote in an early review, Menashe 'compresses thought into language intense and clear as diamonds'. Derek Mahon referred to his art of 'compression and crystallisation'. Both those comments are from 40 years earlier, when Menashe's poetry was briefly noticed in reviews. He was always a solitary figure in American poetry, not writing like anyone else, not part of any clique, not supported by a teaching post and not published for decades.

Born in New York City in 1925, the son of Russian-Jewish immigrant parents, he served in the US infantry during the Second World War. Like Louis Simpson, his most formative and traumatic experience was being a foot soldier in the Battle of the Bulge in 1944-45. He rarely spoke of that time. Again like Simpson, he stayed on in Europe after the war, studying at the Sorbonne in Paris. He returned to New York in the 1950s where, apart from frequent sojourns in Britain, Ireland and Europe, he lived simply in a rent-controlled "cold water" apartment until a year and a half before his death – at the age of 85 – in 2011.

He loved Britain, Ireland and English poetry, and was first published in Britain, thanks to Kathleen Raine's advocacy, in 1961, before he achieved any recognition in America, where he remained a marginal writer for five decades. In 1996 a selection of his work was published in the Penguin Modern Poets series. In 2004 he became the first winner of the Poetry Foundation's Neglected Masters Award, a prize that both paid tribute to his excellence and made reparation for the years when his achievements were overlooked. His *New and Selected Poems*, edited by Christopher Ricks, was published by the Library of America in 2005. After living off next to nothing for most of his life, latterly barely surviving on his war veteran's pension, he found himself holding a cheque for $50,000. It didn't change the habits of a lifetime.

Thanks to Ledbury, he was later published in Britain. That weekend he was staying with Peter and Diana Carter, who put on a lunch for him and other festival guests the day after his reading. Sitting in their garden on a sunny Sunday afternoon, Marina Warner and David Morley were talking poetry and mythology at one end

166

of the table while Samuel regaled me and Pamela Robertson-Pearce with numerous short poems and tales from a long life. Before the lunch was over, I had offered to publish his work, but we wanted to do more than just bring out the American edition over here with Bloodaxe.

In many ways Samuel *was* his poems, or the living embodiment and expression of them, and we wanted readers here to be able to share something like the experience the Ledbury audience had relished on the Saturday and which we'd been privileged to have, one to one, or one to two, on the Sunday. We were going to be in New York that September, and arranged to visit Samuel, to film him talking and saying his poems in the hope of capturing enough footage for a short film.

Samuel had lived on the fifth floor of an apartment block in Thompson Street in Greenwich Village in the same three rooms he'd started renting as a young man over fifty years earlier. His small apartment had never been modernised or even decorated, so the rent was still affordable, but there was no heating or air-conditioning, and no lift. The furniture was basic: a sagging, broken couch; collapsible chairs; and an old bath in the middle of the dusty kitchen area, with a board resting on top to serve as a table. The fridge door hung open, and clearly wasn't used for storing food. But there were oranges perched along the window sills. His only luxury seemed to be freshly laundered cotton shirts: a row of them hung along one wall, evidence, perhaps, that he had spent a few dollars from that Neglected Masters Award which didn't seem to have changed the way he lived in any other way. Books and papers were piled everywhere, mostly in shadowed areas not penetrated by the light from two bare bulbs hanging from the ceiling, but with pride of place on one shelf given to Samuel's Ledbury Poetry Festival 2008 blue bowl keepsake. Pamela took one look at the toilet, and decided against using it.

Yet despite the rundown, dilapidated appearance of the furnishings, what shone brilliantly forth in those shabby rooms was *life* – in the form of a beaming, hospitable and immediately talkative Samuel – and *art*, for virtually every wall was covered from floor to ceiling by huge, wildly different canvases, paintings by artist friends he had been given during the 50s or 60s, mostly by René Brô and David Grossblatt. Home comforts had never meant anything to Samuel: for him, life was about surviving the trauma of war and then living, one day at a time, for freedom, art and poetry.

Living on his own, he only had himself to look after, but suffered in his later years from breathing difficulties brought on by the dust filling the air of Manhattan on 9/11. The World Trade Center was only a few blocks away. With no air-conditioning, windows had to be left open for air, and that air was heavily polluted with dust for weeks afterwards. As a war veteran, Samuel was at least entitled to the free health care he needed in those years, yet every time he left his building for a walk or to go to the shops, he had to climb ten flights of stairs, slowly, catching his breath, step by step.

Our visit was on a sultry morning of heavy rain and thunder, on Tuesday 9 September 2008. With the windows left open for air and lighting less than perfect, conditions weren't ideal, but Samuel gave of his best, working his way through his life and life's work, and talking non-stop for over two hours. With engaging humour, warmth and zest, he recited numerous examples of the poems he knew by heart. Pamela's edited film *Life Is IMMENSE: Visiting Samuel Menashe* includes him saying 44 of those poems, accompanied by much 'warrior wisdom' (to use his phrase) in the framing conversations.

In 2009 Bloodaxe's edition of Samuel's *New & Selected Poems* was published, including Pamela's film on a DVD which comes with the book. If Ledbury was his swansong, this was his final appearance, the book making the best of his work available for the readers in Britain he dearly wanted to connect with, and the film giving everyone the opportunity to see and hear him in the flesh. It still brings him alive to us now. He was delighted when the film was premièred and the book launched at Ledbury Poetry Festival in July 2009, the showing at the Market Theatre attended by many of the friends he had made there the year before.

We huffed and puffed our way up the stairs to his apartment again in September 2009, and did more filming in better conditions, but Samuel, at 84, was more tired. We invited him for a birthday dinner a few days later, along with his lifelong friend and war comrade John Thornton, also in his 80s, whom we immediately warmed to and recognised as a kindred soul. John was his sounding board: they would go for walks every day, often in Central Park; Samuel would say his latest poem and John gave him feedback. Listening to them talking, or arguing even, it was clear that these two war survivors kept each other real and grounded. John also lived simply, in another small apartment, but uptown, on his own, supported, as Samuel had been, by his veteran's pension. But unknown to us, Samuel felt ill as they left the building after our convivial evening, and John had to take him to the hospital.

The following year he finally had to give up his much loved apartment and move into a rest home, but was soon phoning publishers and reading organisers, trying to arrange another trip to England, this time to Cambridge (that never came off), and sending out copies of new poems he wanted to see in print in a new edition or at least in journals. He died in his sleep on 22 August 2011. John Thornton died in 2012.

None of the six late poems by Samuel Menashe included in this anthology appeared in his *New & Selected Poems*, and none has previously been published in Britain. The first poem, 'Reproduce!', was the last he saw published in his lifetime. He told me it made a pair with the second, previously unpublished poem, 'Self Made', which is followed here by another echoing pair of unpublished poems, 'Repose' and 'Awake'. *The Spectator* took a third pair of poems he sent me in 2009, 'Bipolar' and 'The Half of It'. The fifth poem, 'Time Out of Mind', he described as an 'epic', because of its length: he wrote to me about it in December 2009, telling me how he had managed to merge two previously separate poems, 'Bees Busy' and 'Middle Age', and that I should send it to Alan Jenkins for the *TLS*.

As well as speaking his poems to anyone willing to listen, Samuel would write them out on cards or pieces of paper and give them to people. The sixth poem, 'Warm in Wool', is one he included in a card sent to Peter Arscott. It seems right to me that this tribute to Samuel Menashe should finish where it started, in Ledbury, with a poem given to a friend in poetry.

I would like to thank Nicholas Birns for his assistance in compiling this selection, and also Samuel's cousin, Herbert Weisberg.

ADRIAN MITCHELL

My Literary Career So Far

As I prowled through Parentheses
I met an Robin and a Owl
My Grammarboots they thrilled like bees
My Vowelhat did gladly growl

Tis my delight each Friedegg Night
To chomp a Verbal Sandwich
Scots Consonants light up my Pants
And marinade my Heart in Language

Alphabet Soup was all my joy!
From Dreadfast up to Winnertime
I swam, a naked Pushkinboy
Up wodka vaterfalls of rhyme

And reached the summit of Blue Howl
To find a shining Suit of Words
And joined an Robin and a Owl
In good Duke Ellington's Band of Birds

December 18, 2008

Merry Crambo and a Hippy New Year
        with love from

Adrian Mitchell, The Shadow Poet Laureate

(I can't write letters and it's hard to phone yer as I recover from two months'
in Pneumonia so take this new riff with a glass of good wine and drink to Peace
in 2009)

Adrian Mitchell (1932-2008) was a great favourite at Ledbury Poetry Festival.
This was the last poem he wrote, sent as a Christmas greeting to friends and
family. He died two days later.

ANNE MICHAELS

Ask Aloud

To taste the salt of the stars
in the sea. To love another
more than oneself. To know this
is to know everything.

Do you see how the dusk and rain
are one?

Do our bodies come to nothing?

Not how we fall in love,
but how we fail in love.

Ask aloud what comes of us.

My love, do you understand me?
Not surmise
but sunrise.

Ask aloud what comes of us.

KEI MILLER

The Weight of Bees
(for LC)

I knew a woman who once placed her head
Under a tap of water, and said – Kei,
look at me,
I weigh 400 pounds, I can't hide.

And she said it as if pounds
Was the same as years, like she was saying
I weigh 400 years – as if hers
was the weight of history,
of canefields, the brutal Atlantic.
You wonder what kind of man could make
A woman feel so bad bout sheself,
Could leave her numb by a tap of water
Considering how she might fit herself
Down the drain. I wanted to say,
O daughter of Zion, lift up your head
for thou art comely; I wanted to say
yours is another weight completely –
yours is the weight of love and livity.
400 pounds is the approximate weight
of 20,000 hibiscuses, or the weight
of one million, two hundred and ninety-five thousands
bees

REZA MOHAMMADI   ■ AFGHANISTAN / IRAN

Illegal Immigrant

it is possible
the sun has risen
and over the mountains
the clouds are there still,
that winds are driving
and families arriving
and there is the sound of a party
sound of dancing, chanting,
and glasses smashing,
the laughter exploding
in every minute and people
and happiness and also

me, with my big heart,
in a ship or strapped under
the truck, I am crossing
the border and moment
by moment am entering
with glory England

translated from the Dari by Nick Laird & Hamid Kabir

KIM MOORE

The Scaffolder

He says his hands are the worst. He's lost his grip.
Years of working without gloves when he was young.

He'd wait for the hot aches, then the pins and needles
and once they'd come, he knew he'd be all right,

could work all day and his hands would just stay numb.
Now the cold turns the ends of his fingers white.

His first fall from a house roof, he swears the building
shrugged him off. A broken hip and when it set

one leg shorter than the other. Back ache for thirty years.
And who's to say it wasn't luck the second time

that dropped him thirty feet and gave him broken ribs,
a knock to the head that made his temper strange.

Sometimes when he picks things up they drop.
The other day it was a cup. Just slipped right through

his fingers. The last time he fell, he thought he was done,
but there's always the sky that whispers *up, go up.*

BLAKE MORRISON

Meredith

'I began with poetry and I shall finish with it.'

The strange low sobs that shook their common bed
Were a secret like creation or the stars.
He didn't breathe a word till she was dead.

He hoped she'd grow to love him when they wed
But the sweetness of her kisses soon turned sour
As strange low sobs consumed their common bed

She played the loyal wife while guests were fed
And listened as he talked – blah–blah–di–blah.
She knew she'd have no life till he was dead.

Until a handsome painter turned her head.
Together they performed a *coup d'état*.
New passions rocked the dull old marriage bed.

He took to writing novels when she fled.
He knew she'd not come back but nor stray far.
Alone and undivorced, she soon was dead.

The thing was so much worse than people said.
You had to read his books to see the scars.
The strange low sobs that shook their common bed.
The tale he only told when she was dead.

■ I've fond memories of coming to Ledbury when Ruth Padel was the poet in residence – Wimbledon was on in the background (these were Henman rather than Murray days) and I talked about my namesake, William Blake. One of the outstanding poetry festivals. I hope to visit it again one day. [BM]

SINÉAD MORRISSEY

The Rope
(after Michael Longley)

I have paused in the door-jamb's shadow to watch you
        playing Shop or Cliff! or Café or Under-the-Sea
among the flotsam of props on our tarmacked driveway.
        All courtship. All courtesy.

At eight and six, you have discovered yourselves friends,
        at last, and this the surprise the summer
has gifted me, as if some
        penny-cum-handkerchief conjuror

had let loose a kingfisher…
        You whirl and pirouette, as in a ballet,
take decorous turns, and pay for whatever you need
        with a witch's currency:

grass cuttings, sea glass, coal, an archaeopteryx
        of glued kindling from the fire basket;
you don two invisible outsize overcoats – for love?
        for luck? – and jump with your eyes shut.

And I can almost see it thicken between you,
        your sibling-tetheredness, an umbilicus,
fattened on mornings like this as on a mother's blood,
        loose, translucent, not yet in focus,

but incipient as yeast and already strong enough
        to knock both of you off your balance
when you least expect it, some afternoon after work,
        decades hence,

one call from a far-flung city and, look,
        all variegated possibles – lovers, kids, apartments –
whiten into mist; the rope is flexing,
        tugging you close and you come, obedient

children that you are, back to this moment,
        staggering to a halt and then straightening,
little again inside your oversize coats and shoes
            and with sea glass still to arrange, but without me watching.

HELEN MORT

Mountain

You are very successful
but you have rocks in your chest,

skin-coloured sandstone
wedged where your breasts should be.

Your stomach is a boulder.
To hold you up, your legs grow stony too.

You zip your jacket up
and nobody notices you are a mountain.

You buy coffee,
run board meetings where no one says

you are dry rock
but above your head, their talk is weather,

your eyes collect new rain
and you know what you are because

like any hillside
you don't sleep. Your feet could hold you here

forever but your sides
are crumbling, and when you speak

your words are rockfall, you're
scared your heart is tumbling from your mouth.

ANDREW MOTION

The Elimination of a Picture
Richard Dadd 1817-1886

A philosopher of the Medway
    Richard Dadd senior
was struck on the head then stabbed
      with a five   inch folding rigger's knife
        while answering a call of nature
at the edge of a deep dell circled with elm trees
    by his son Richard Dadd junior
        the painter
who afterwards tidied the body
    and buttoned the coat
      before bolting to France.

      Here he was arrested
after attacking a fellow-passenger on a coach
    when two stars in Ursa Major
      swam closer together
and in this way delivered an instruction
        from Osiris.

    In Bedlam and subsequently Broadmoor
greatly preoccupied by the existence of a second self
    Richard Dadd worked on his masterpiece
    The Fairy Feller's Masterstroke
with a bag of acid drops on one side of his easel
    and on the other
      the copy of a favourite classical text.

      These two pictures are like monks
    and apparently say very little
      about the condition of their creator
except his loss of a shared human scale.

Yet what is more slavish than painting.

What
                he asks himself
    what is more hopeless.

Surrounded by a delirium of description
    including daisies
           wide-eyed although it is night-time
towering stalks of Timothy grass
        and a whole community of freaks and oddballs
the Fairy Feller unbuttons his brown top coat
      steadies his mind by pressing down his hat
          then raises his miniature axe
only to discover the double-spread of the blade
      is the one patch of canvas Dadd has left unfinished.

Therefore he is not able to deliver his stroke.

PAUL MULDOON

With Eilmer of Malmesbury

(in memory of Jack Eustis, 1998-2014)

In Paddington a man allows his upright bass
to rest its head on his shoulder –
the awkward embrace
of a father and teenage son. I think of one who smoulders

in a flame as I take the train
to Swindon, from there a cab to the Old Bell hotel,
the oldest in England. Since the unusually large brain
of an Apache war chief will swell

even more when boiled, an army surgeon saws
through Mangas's brain-stem, tipping it into a vermeil
basin for further study. It was from watching jackdaws
avail of the thermals

over this scarp that Eilmer got it into his head he might
take off from the church tower.
This was in 1000 AD, or thereabouts, so his flight
was a testimony to Eilmer's staying power

even though he went no more than two hundred yards.
He fell, broke both legs, and was 'lame ever after'.
My friends' beloved son also fell hard
from a rafter

but stopped short
of the floor. An 11th century Benedictine monk
was given a daily allowance of a quart
of soup in which to dunk

bread made from barley and spelt.
We don't know if Eilmer flew with the aid of feathers
or a contraption of linen and silk. The belt
worn by a Benedictine was made of leather

but a Franciscan's cincture was rope. The gaudy sleeve
I once put on is fraying by the hour.
At a distance of three thousand miles I grieve
with my friends. An E minor on a bass sours

even as it soars through the skull of Mangas Colorado.
When I look down I see the pall cast over everything
is only partly the shadow
of my own wing.

TOGARA MUZANENHAMO ZIMBABWE

+49

He could not deny it, +49 was beautiful.
He stood at the porthole studying the ship pulsing in the light.
The craft. Black. Huge. Hanging like a lizard hibernating in oil.
Its belly intricately overlaid – dark tiny scales throwing a chrome
washed glow, soft, almost invisible; its skin translating starlight
                    into ancient psalms of the spectrum.

Again the blue light shot off her stern.
Arcing wide. Drawing in before shooting out into the distance
like a beacon from a lighthouse. Every hour or so a pod emerged
from her hull, each pod identical in shape. The crafts hung beneath
+49, surrounded by the thin mist – silver pearls at first glance
                    glowing with the indifference of death.

There was a deep philosophy in +49's presence.
From the quiet image he saw – he knew the horrific soughs
it threw when the blue light turned grey. The chaos before the silence.
Every thought falling away to cease. In the craft's wake – a faint
rainbow peeled off its scales. The light, a wet black slough
                    beneath the wings of this unholy giant.

DALJIT NAGRA

The day Heaney died

Floor spots on the end-night of a poetry course
then the last student whose performance signals
we follow him off the sofas,
            who strides out the barn, as if possessed,
            crossing the Totleigh stones to recite,
what would you seek from without?

180

We're led by his torch over grass that wears
upright water, though we're some way behind
    and hear him
        · in flits, *out here*
bare space is home to the yawning cow...
One of the sixteen, overwhelmed by wet feet
and the squelch below, sounds cheerful enough,
I think I've lost my foot in a cowpat.

    We rise up the still-warm hill
where our guide seems, on the brow, apparitional,
who glows us a lane to his hearth
then ends pleading, *Is not the air inspired*
    by another place, another life?

Have we been dragged by the grunts,
    the gutturals of our flesh,
tied to the customary rhythms of verse
in the valley of our own passive assent
for the usual let-downs? Except when his torch blanks,
    we are bulled into darkness.
Our instinct is to elevate our heads
    and seek out a luminous speck
so we gasp to state we're upon a harvest
    of stars, a cascade heaven.
Lost for a moment in the loosening gravity.

Till there, beyond the silence of breath
the brightest by far,
    the one in the line of the great glow
        like the first light of the soul
        that's become its own source,
a pilot to the host, the lost, the grief-sore:

    North.

■ The year I was at the festival, I was introduced to a tall pale man in his 30s
who had a shaven head, tight trousers and black boots. He looked for all the
world like some gung-ho BNP devotee.
    Yet when he spoke he had a foreign accent and he smiled to meet me.

Maybe it was my relief at not being escorted down a Ledbury alley but I instantly liked him. It turned out he was an Estonian poet, and whilst he had very little English and I had no Estonian, we shared a few pints in the pub and exchanged books. His book was illustrated on every page.

I remember the front cover of his hardback had a large black bird with angry eyes. I faintly recall the whole book being full of humans and animals sucking blood or copulating in cumbersome postures. I have lost the book and did not keep in touch with the Estonian poet but I loved meeting him. That was my only and only tangible contact with Estonia. I suspect these chance meetings only happen in relaxed poet-friendly festivals such as Ledbury. [DN]

KATRINA NAOMI

Maybe Owls
(for J.S.)

The birds in the silver birches listened
as we shone our light over rock
jutting through the moss and grass
of the path. The night silenced us,
we became aware of the still sky
and the stars we were ignorant of.
The need for concentration was there
for the cliff fell away to our left.
At the bend in the path, the birds
took their chance – screeched and flapped
at us, as if we were intruders,
as if we had no right to the dark.
You grasped my arm, my hair,
as you forced my arm over your shoulder
and cowered – an awkward half-kneel,
the torch beam making an involuntary cross
against the woods. I've never known a man
make me hug him. For an instant
I considered if this was all a pretence –
your ornithophobia – but the birds

must have been pleased at their work
for you opened your mouth and screamed,
almost an enjoyment in the pitch of it.
And again – that release.
I used my in-control voice, steady
and slightly stern, which also came
of its own volition. I heard my words,
considered them and our many selves,
considered again the shelter you took
and how the stars didn't recognise us either,
and the night went on, knowingly.
Under my command, we walked back,
faster than we'd come. And you let my arm go.
Stood apart. And I thought, later, maybe owls,
with their whiteness, their bright moon faces,
and how quickly the quiet folded the sounds
away, blending them into the dark, the night
mending itself, the sounds carried
by the river and away down the valley.

■ I won the Ledbury Poetry Festival Text Poem Competition back in 2008. It
was the first competition that I was placed in. It really encouraged me. I went
on to have my first book published later that year. Thank you. [KN]

AMJAD NASSER ■ JORDAN / UK

Light

During her final days, which we sort of knew would be her final
days, since cancer rarely pulls a prank, and the eyes of farewell
often don't postpone what they want to stay today for tomorrow,
my mother, watching me prepare my suitcase for the departure I
came from and to which I'd return, said in supplication: May God
light your way. In what I heard I immediately saw the Verse of
Light, written in complicated Kufic script, hanging on the wall:

'God is the Light of the heavens and the earth, the parable of His Light is as if there were a Niche and within it a Lamp, the Lamp enclosed in Glass, the Glass as if it were a brilliant star lit up by a blessed Tree, an Olive neither of the East or of the West, whose Oil is Luminous, without being touched by flame: Light upon Light...'.

In which darkness did my mother see my walk so that she'd spend a few more of the precious words she had remaining in her account? What did her eyes that gleamed with the glow of extinguished silver see as she was peering into the afterlife?

It was daylight.

The sun had granted creatures amplified shadows.

An old saluki dog sat panting under a eucalyptus tree.

Pebbles were incandescent in a dry riverbed.

It was no ordinary light that which my mother wished to illuminate my path. It wasn't Edison's light bulb, or fluorescent, luminescent light, or the light of projectors at football stadiums, or that of the space shuttle's orbiter. It wasn't Shakespeare's pendulum in no man's land, between light and lightness. It wasn't even the Pharisee torch that Christ set aside. My mother meant *Noor*. Although she was likely ignorant of the argument that still rages on in Arabic about the difference between the two lights, *Noor* and *Dao* (and the extended irony in transliteration).

Astronomers, obsessed with their observatories and mathematics, say there is no scientific difference between *Noor* and *Dao*, that they are no more than poetic wordplay. But Sufis claim a difference that observatories can't detect and math can't comprehend. God, the Light of heaven and earth, doesn't need to resort to a game of words and meaning to resemble poetry. Yet even so, there is no harm if *Noor* is poetry and *Dao* is prose, since the latter has numerous sources, and dances according to supply and demand. The former, however, like poetry, is rare. If and when it is revealed to one, that person will survive many an unseen darkness. And the veil may even be lifted, and one becomes a saint.

Years passed since my mother's death. I no longer resemble my Bedouin ancestors and look to the stars during my stays and travels. For all I know, only batteries and electric companies have lit my way.

It's clear, for reasons I can guess, that God did not fulfil my mother's prayer.

All this came to mind while I was trying, unsuccessfully, to write a poem about a greenish light, lime luminosity, limelight, citric light that leaves no shadow of an outstretched hand or a body walking in its domain.

Is remembering my mother a pretext to write about *Noor/Dao*, or is writing about them a pretext to remember my mother?

Dao will be the last thing humans see.
The origin
is the dark.

Behind his shut lids
a child sees *dao*.
The first thing wasn't a scream.

When we turn off *dao*
the jet-black night isn't faraway.
In a flash it returns.

Under a green moon-*dao*
I extend my hand.
A willow branch shakes.

Stars and planets
aren't lanterns for our sake.
They have other tasks.

The Yemeni Sirius
is in his constellation.
An abandoned God.

Without *dao* there is no colour.
Black and white
are a division of labour.

Dao and shadow are side by side
as long as
we remain earth-bound.

Purity.
Before this visual contamination.
Your face.

Although *noor*
is essence it is
also form.

The humility
of *noor*'s essence turns it
into form.

When you are in the land of *noor*
take off your footwear
walk barefoot as you were born.

Noor is a laughing face.
A hand waving from a distance.
Memory of mother.

translated from the Arabic by Fady Joudah

GRACE NICHOLS   ■ GUYANA / UK

Night

You who always come flooding back
in the shades of your original form –

186

But shot through now
with street lights and neon –
a glitzy black mother of pearl

Dressed in black olive
                    and onyx
drinking dark chocolate
                    and licorice
at the trendy Café Noir.

You who can reverse yourself
and light is born.

But I remember when you
were simply a dark astonishment
that allowed fireflies and stars to glow
as I star-gazed with my brother
at childhood's window

And you yourself bent down low
to harbour us in your arms.

TAL NITZÁN
■ ISRAEL

A Short History

No one among us recalls any more
how long we've been waiting
for a blind white wave to expunge that whose
mere resurrected memory
could clench the chest in the morning,
the trachea at night

For, the ant swarms which were driven away
return to blacken our homes, and boiling water

from the porcelain cups leaps into our faces,
and knives which have grown weary by berry flesh
are seeking fingers.

When will the scraps of paper flying about subside,
the shreds of a futile spell
sink into dust?

What sounded like rain was just building waste
piled up to a mound.
What sounded like wailing was wailing.
For some time now we've been in need of a new disaster
to destroy the remains of our disaster.

translated from the Hebrew by Aliza Raz

KIWAO NOMURA ■ JAPAN

And then parade

1

And so,
The sky feels itchy,
I'd considered everything in turn very carefully,
And so, no light gets in,
The sky feels itchy,
Is it because of my skin, hee hee hee,
A good, funny shout,
I stretched and stretched this way that way,
Humming's a grass,
And so, and so,
Oh no, I've left my bones somewhere,
The sky feels itchy,

2

Seven minutes to madness,
The insects have started to move,

3

In the back of the brain, the rice field ridges, ridge after ridge, among old lonely nerve bushes, I thought it must be something like a grain, and it shook, maybe shaken by the wind, and concentrating my attention, as if drawn by my attention, it began to move, coming this way, no longer a grain, an insect, what can I do? in the outside world I would either squash the insect or leave, that would be it, but in the back of the brain, and not just one, at first there was one, but now it seems like a whole nest, bubbling up, repellent, there's nothing I can do,

4

Insects, and more insects,
It's practically
The same as,
Considering everything in turn very carefully

5

The leading group already across the ninth ridge,
Gradually growing in size,
Shrieking of nectar,
Shrieking of winged robes,
They're like rope,
Rope all over,
World-scale rope,
Shredded, squeezed,

6

Insects seeing insects and saying
We're all eye,
Insects hearing insects and saying
We're all ear,
Insects saying if touched by insects
We'd be all hand,
None separate,
None vanish,

189

7

And then again,
Large-scale insects, like swaying industrial complexes,
Then insects drowning in blood at rest,
Then insects formed entirely of the bones of voice,

8

It can't be helped, I must
Imagine a wall slightly in front of the back of the brain,
In case the insects come,

9

And so,
I should like to state that I have, just today, drawn a line under
    that, period,
The future coming round and round,
And so, I scratch,
Pastures inside,
Depth of skin, not yet come, distant and familiar,
Wiping the slate clean, fiercely wiping the slate clean,
Holding underarm the wave of a laugh about something remembered,
Scratch, scratch,
And so,
I should like to state that I have, just today, drawn a line under that,
    period,
The future coming round and round,

10

An insect like the period,
Flies up, floats up from the ridge,
Fin, fellow,
Filly, fissure,
This way, that way, and then,
As if saying
Straight ahead, that's obvious,
Lands on the next ridge
And looks back

11

And then again,
Insects suddenly called by name,
Or perhaps bubbles emptily calling the names,
Insects like the bubbles,
Or perhaps towers spouting viscous bubbles,
Insects like the towers,
Swarming, swarming,
Insects, whatever,
Insects, whatever,

12

Repellent, there's nothing I can do, the leading party will soon reach the wall, if only they would turn back, if they start climbing, no they can't, it's steep and slip slippery, no thought can climb, however carefully things are considered in turn, so neither will the insects, no that's not right, somewhere they may've become more insect, may just abandon thought, and then they'll climb without caring that it's a wall, when that happens, I, when that happens I

13

Ma, mamaamu,
Sound insects,
Hamu, ma, maamu,
Sound insects,
Maamu, mama, Mysterious,

14

Three minutes to madness,
The insects have started to climb the wall,

translated from the Japanese by Angus Turvill

VÍCTOR RODRÍGUEZ NÚÑEZ

from **stopover**

5 [Powell's Books]

that flower with history
won't make this qasida smell any better
the stone dreamt by the jeweller
won't brighten it

this is written on the tree bark
gone missing in the forest
to subtract chances?
                          to add essences?

there's no formula for this yeast
everything takes shape freehand
                                      eyeballing

inspiration is a zero to the left
this is written in the mould
                          not in the rock

8 [Helen's Sewing Room]

the house blessed by silk
in a wicker taboret
prayers in ribbon
                  calm the north

flowers stamped on the wall
to perfume sleep with musk
patterns and measures
                      error discarded

soaks the fabric
at the foot of the scissor rainbow
no door shuts

      vigil half-closed
everything in a meticulous mess
the world to mend

12 [Oregon City]

between a bluebird jumping from the grass
with the first light
         and a verse by Szymborska
against the mix ups of death

you have a lingering doubt
           its rustproof stem
its geometric corolla
the rubble runs to seed

        at the hands of the dew
its stubborn celestial thirst
         the rhyme from another world

meaningless signifier
every thing a voice
       with nothing to say

translated from the Spanish by Katherine M. Hedeen

NAOMI SHIHAB NYE

Good Night, Sleep Tight
(for Billy Collins)

They thought we were married in Michigan, Billy,
telling me my husband's books had sold out while mine
still loitered in the shelves.
My husband has no books, I said, perplexed.
Later you announced from the stage
we have the perfect marriage,
we hardly ever get together.

But that's not true. We do. Everywhere,
we're following the same air.
I go where you've been,
a year or more behind you.
Cobbles of Church Lane in Ledbury,
sweetness of hourly bells.
We sleep, adjacent years,
same house in Helsinki,
same salty inn by Katchemak Bay, Alaska.

Everyone tells me what you did everywhere.
And you're so much braver.
Today I pass the Prince of Wales pub you probably entered.
They say the kitchen closed three minutes ago.
I'm sure it was open when you were here, Billy.
Am I a shadow twin, is there
a quiet space between your perfect stanzas
big enough to live in?
The extra pocket in your jacket,
the fringe, on the cliff and near the sea,
it's less lonely knowing you're out there,
but where are you today? I'll make my plan.
And no, I did not fly your tiny prop plane gazing for bears in Homer,
nor rent a kayak for an otter glide, I did not book a car in England
to drive on the left of the skinny road.
I have little to show. I watered the plants.
And listened to fabulous poets.

Billy, we're so lucky.
Good thing no competitive streak simmers under this lid.
But today a friendly tear rose in my eye to leave Ledbury.
I'll bet I loved this place even more than you did.

Life Loves

to change, wrote John Masefield, after growing up
in the cobbled town of Ledbury, Herefordshire.
   Precise crosswalks, Saturday markets,
droning church bells persist with conviction.
A man called Ledbury one of the few 'real towns' left
   in England, meaning – sad to say – they don't have
      many immigrants.   Too bad, for it was easy to imagine
changing everything, hiding out down Cottage Lane
   in the garden of massive white roses for more than one season,
toting a bottle of Fusty Ferret Ale to the garden table
   along with a paper-wrapped hunk of greasy fish and chips
from a nameless shack down an alley, where the mayor
   told me to go. Who knows how many lives
long for us in our fading diminishment? We're
      still rich with appetite for a cider shop's thirty faucets,
      a tiny courtyard sprouting herbs.
Haunting the print shop, plucking sheaves
   of discarded margins from rubbish bin –
      long thin creamy strips – basking
         in disgusted teen chatter on the green
by the graveyard, enjoying the air.
   It became my air too quickly.
And then I had to leave, still thinking of Masefield,
   a poet who suffered intense seasickness yet wrote about
      going down to the sea as if it were his favorite act.
Onto a packed train, across an entire region, then an ocean,
   guzzling window views like some desperate addict
      who says, underneath every – This is mine now
and I love it –
   I will die, I will die, I will die.

SEAN O'BRIEN

Storm Beach

It feels like an achievement, emptiness
Reorganised to make the matter plain.
In the long pool trapped behind the shingle bank

The sky is blue and bitter. Amstel crates
And ragged scalps of weed have likewise
Been reconsidered, while the sea

Has gone somewhere as if for good:
No distance has been spared
And the horizon is revealed as yet another

Obsolescent form of measurement,
Leaving only the sublime
By which to take a sunblind bearing.

It's freezing when we stroll onstage –
We find the rake is steeper now –
As if at last we ought to broach

The fundamentals wisely put aside
Long since in weatherproof compartments
For such as day as this. But instantly it's clear

That ours will not be speaking parts.
The gulls will do all that. In this austerity
Of blazing salt-charged air and stunned geology

We're only here to represent the crowd
Who cross and go to do the greeting
And the mourning, further on and further out.

BERNARD O'DONOGHUE

Salmon
(for Andrew McNeillie)

It was rumoured that in the local river
that flowed so lightly, shallow, at the bottom
of our land, there were deep holes, especially
Poll a' Cúinne, the hole at the corner
where the river bent and then bent back again,
working out its course towards the village.
It was said too that in those dangerous depths
there had lived for many years a salmon
that all the local fishermen competed
to capture. Was it for him the poacher's glow
kept vigil in the dark night, out of season,
when we watched out of the bathroom window?
And was it him that Dan Joe Quinn wordlessly
brought to us, wrapped in the *Examiner*,
held in place by the bicycle's spring carrier?
And was the wisdom that he kept from us
the knowledge that Dan Joe's wife was soon
to die, leaving him in sole, sorrowful charge?

SHARON OLDS

A Mercy

It seemed, to me, a mercy, that he died
'without a mark on him'. I don't
remember who told me that, maybe one of his
roommates, who'd been in the car with him,
and who'd come through unscathed. A month later,

summer, they came to my home town, we drank
Paisano, and smoked Abdullahs,
oval and pastel as Easter baskets
(the morning of the accident).
And last night, I heard the word
windshield, and I suddenly wondered
how he could have been thrown free of the
car, to end up, curled up
on the verge, dead, without a mark on him.
And then for a moment I almost saw but I
would not see him, fontanelle
first, being born up out of the glass
into his fresh new death, his first
not breath, not heartbeat. And it seemed, to me –
though it was not – like evil, for his
young head to be scribbled on,
defaced. But then I brought the shards
back together above the dash,
I drew in the lines of the spider-line cracks,
and mended the car and him and brought him,
whole, back down behind the wheel,
and when he swerved, and hit something,
his door opened, and he flew out,
asleep, his arms cradling his head,
and he fell to earth, and slept on the grass
for the rest of his life.

FRANK ORMSBY

The Willow Forest

What with the pogroms, the genocide,
the ethnic cleansing, the secret massacres,
the mass graves, the death camps, the public executions,
at last there was nobody left,

the country was empty.
Survivors who reached the borders
became refugees.

Rebuked by that silence beyond the mountains,
the victors planted willows and in due course
the country grew into a willow forest.
The trees hung their heads
over a history that, now memorialised,
could be forgotten.

Except that the few who visited
spoke of a weight
that was more than gravity,
a wind in the trees
that stilled to a kind of weeping.

LEANNE O'SULLIVAN ■ IRELAND

David Copperfield

No, no finer thing than to walk through town
with the key of my house in my pocket,
to stop to talk with women and men
of all the easeful talk of cures and debts.

And all the while to know its nickel backed,
winter light turning warm in my hand,
the strike of the bolt-stump, my footing exact
as though I could dream-walk myself back

to stand in the dark of the inner door –
no answer save my own – then gently
lever its weight toward the bright rooms. Oh, hoard
of the free life! Of the sunlit, scattering plenty.

RUTH PADEL

Encontro das Águas

It is unlike anything else. Wild swimming,
the nub of selves meeting, conflux
of two rivers, the dark and the gold,

Rio Negro and Rio Solimões in Brazil.
The kiss. Nerve-ends, twisting together
underground. Each name touched

and forgotten, in a *time-really-can-stand-still*
that makes us shiver. No more Durga,
She-Who-is-Difficult-to-Reach –

we are a whole shaman's journey in ourselves.
An invisible bridge, quest to the interior.
Any *what-do-you-think-of-me*'s

dissolve in each other's dark. A promise
that may never be fulfilled
but is complete, each moment, in itself.

■ When I first arrived at Ledbury Poetry Festival, I knew I'd come to poetry heaven. A folded green landscape, radiating memories of older poets and writers. A festival headquarters in a gorgeous 16th-century building, which turned out to be the registry office where it was thought W.H. Auden had married Thomas Mann's daughter.* A town so passionate about poetry they had banded together to start a poetry festival and were hosting poets in their own homes.

One year, I had to have stitches taken out of my leg while I was there. In the cottage hospital, the nurse who took them out told me her children adored the festival: wonderful poets came to their school – they were all doing "poetry things". Another year, when I was a Poet in Residence and taught a week of workshops, I stayed in the Carters' hospitable and venerable house. Getting to know them, their glowing garden and their green valley, and through them the festival's human history, was unforgettable.

Here's to Ledbury, hieroglyph of English landscape which mingles poetry traditions effortlessly with cutting-edge international poetry – and the next twenty years. [RP]

* [Auden's wedding actually took place at the former Registry Office in Bank Crescent.]

BRIAN PATTEN

The Minister for Exams

When I was a child I sat an exam.
The test was so simple.
There was no way I could fail.

Q1. Describe the taste of the Moon.

It tastes like Creation I wrote,
it has the flavour of starlight.

Q2. What colour is Love?

Love is the colour of the water a man
lost in the desert finds, I wrote.

Q3. Why do snowflakes melt?

I wrote, they melt because they fall
on to the warm tongue of God.

There were other questions.
They were just as simple.

I described the grief of Adam when he was expelled from Eden.
I wrote down the exact weight of an elephant's dream.

Yet today, many years later,
For my living I sweep the streets
or clean out the toilets of the fat hotels.

Why? Because constantly I failed my exams.
Why? Well, let me set a test.

Q1. How large is a child's imagination?
Q2. How shallow is the soul of the Minister for Exams?

PASCALE PETIT

My Wolverine

When my mother says I was her kit
taken from her too early,
I think not of cats but a wolverine,
my devourer of snowfields, who,
when she can find no more prey,
eats herself, even the frozen bones.
I crawl down the black phone line
as if it's an umbilicus
to the last refuge on our planet,
towards whatever back country
happens to be her territory today.
My nails remember to claw.
I lope up the icefall
she's retreated to, that's melting behind her
as she climbs her precipice, too drunk
on freedom to come down.
She shows me the den where words are born
fighting. I do not blame her.
I hold the receiver against my face
as if it's her muzzle, her reek
of blizzard-breath. I embrace
the backward-barbed teeth that can
fell a moose and gnaw even its hooves.
Kit – she spits the word out
in a half-love half-snarl and I
am her glutton, scavenging on my yelp
when I was torn from her after birth,
and again now – not long before she dies.

■ I will never forget my first reading at Ledbury, it was the first time I had read at a festival. I decided to read from my second collection *The Zoo Father*, while I was still writing it, and I had to read for a whole hour on my own, 10am on a Sunday morning. I didn't sleep at all the previous night. But as I read these exposing poems filled with Amazonian imagery and animals, about my dark childhood, to the packed hall, I realised the audience were with me, were listening intently. I thought my poems were too brutal for a Sunday morning, but they seemed to like them so much that they bought every copy of my first collection afterwards and I was very encouraged to finish writing my second book. Ledbury is special to me because of this and I am always delighted to return, each time it's an affirming, happy experience, rather dream-like. Ledbury is a festival where poetry is treated as serious fun, everyone there works very hard to create the right atmosphere for each poet's world. [PP]

CLARE POLLARD

In the Horniman Museum

In South London, on a Sunday,
we have seen the scratching chickens
and alpacas being spitty
when the rain drives us indoors
where the taxidermy's waiting
and you race around glass coffins,
the hummingbirds in friezes,
Vulpes vulpes and the *Cervus*
posed like toys in toyshop windows
and the walrus like a punchline.
They are animals, as you are –
relation of *Pan troglodytes* –
each captured by a caption
in a tea trader's collection.
He paid to have the world paused:
all those thousand conscious seeings
for one vision! All that *I am*
turned to glaze for one man's gaze.

I've not told you about death yet.
Can you tell these birds are different?
Do you think this heron cruel,
that he doesn't care about you?

It's true. The heron doesn't.
Caring's something rare and fleeting
(if the dead see anything
then it's as hard and black as glass.)
But your eyes are getting rounder,
pointing 'dere!' at crocs and gibbons
and the peacock's staring blueness,
and we're falling through our days
in this pissing useless ark
while the clouds gather like stuffing,
while the water's ticking upwards.

My child, you are an *I*.
Through your two eyes, not yet dark,
can you see your wet-cheeked mother
and the whole creaturely Kingdom
as they stand today before you
in their opulence and armour,
who have held their breath this moment
and are waiting for your judgement?

■ I was still a very young poet, my debut collection *The Heavy-Petting Zoo* just
out, when I was first invited to Ledbury and it was thrilling. It felt like I was
part of the poetry world for the first time. I was put up in the same house as
Sean O'Brien! And then my first green room! I remember staying up late on
the last night, drinking with Yang Lian and Jack Mapanje as they sang folk songs,
thinking I was in literary heaven. [CP]

JACOB POLLEY

Jackself's Quality

        can't be bought
or stolen   Mudder hasn't bottled it
   Mugginshere hasn't brought it home
in his briefcase

the farmer hasn't clipped its weighty foam
from his blackest sheep
    the hawk-man, with a rag of meat
in his leather glove, can't bring it
stooping from the sky   Thomascat
hasn't fetched it from the farmyard
to lay still warm at Jackself's feet
the dark continent
Jackself peels from the flank
of a Friesian cow, ties to his ankles
and drags across the flatland
at midday, doesn't prove
his substance   the night
is made of what he needs
    he moonwalks in daylight,
afraid like snow he'll wane or drift
before he can hold
the road out front, the fields behind
and the earth in the churchyard
    so Jackself crawls to the coal-shed
and eats

KATRINA PORTEOUS

The Ain Sakhri Lovers

Little bean, twin cotyledon, lips ajar –
He is embracing her, or she him.
Their faces are hidden from us. His knees,
Arched under hers, open her, a flower.

How beautiful they are, flawless, nameless,
Older than writing, than building, and tender
And delicate; for he has taken root
In her, or she in him, and they are gone

Into the greater, all-embracing stillness.
Born out of the one grain, they are a secret
Known only to each other, almost worn
Back to the pebble, polished, smoothed in water,

Or deep in the furrow, or on the plain's tongue –
And plucked, for this moment, out of the long river.

This carving, found in a cave in the Judean desert and now in the British
Museum, is 11,000 years old and dates from the beginnings of agriculture. It
is the earliest known depiction of a couple making love.

■ On the 300 mile train journey from Northumberland, I thought of Wilfred
Gibson, the Northumbrian poet who settled near Ledbury a century ago.
Gibson sought the company of the Dymock Poets, Rupert Brooke, Robert
Frost and Edward Thomas, whose feelings for rural life distinguished them
before World War I. That he felt the need for a literary community, while
writing what was somewhat condescendingly referred to as "people's poetry",
contained a massive tension. The implicit questions – who and what is poetry
for? What place has the countryside in evolving English culture? – remain
acutely relevant. In Ledbury's medieval market setting I reflected on some
common cultural distinctions: South and North, metropolitan and rural, "literary"
and "popular". I was a long way from home, but the festival – its celebratory
atmosphere, packed readings in the Burgage Hall, sandwiches and chatter in
the green room, the volunteers' kindness and hospitality – briefly gave me a
sense of belonging, immersion in a community of poets – an invaluable, nec-
essarily impermanent, gift to take back into everyday life. [KP]

CRAIG RAINE

Bitch

This Weimaraner in Spandex,
tight on the deep chest,
webbed at the tiny waist.

The drips and drabs of her dugs:
ten, a tapering wedge,
narrowed towards the back legs.

She gives me her paw,
a branch with buds, four
spare pads and claws.

Her tail's unstoppable verve
and swerve,
the long hard curve

of a skipping rope.
Metronomic, rapid,
slow, three-speed raps.

Each ear an evening dress
cut on the bias.
The golden eyes pious

(praying for food).
She poos
like a kangaroo.

And eats like a washing machine.
The lavish eight-inches-long
shoe-shop-shoehorn tongue.

Hunger: her muzzle's
cribbage board a drizzle
of glycerin spittle.

She sleeps as if
she were a penknife,
legs half-folded away. Twitched off.

As the Past Approaches

As the past approached,
the future, even when you've lived it,
remains to be seen.
Behind that door
there is life. But guess!
Out or in?
This side or the other?
Closed or open?
Who's waiting for me there?
Who am I waiting for?
I have still to discover.
One foot forward,
one backward.
The truth is
neither key nor lock.

translated from the Hindi by Bernard O'Donoghue & Lucy Rosenstein

BRENDA READ-BROWN

How to make an angel smile

If there were angels,
this is where they would live,
or somewhere like this;
not frozen in a gloomy church,
stuffed with sin;
not weeping in a graveyard,

waiting for the end to begin;
not standing at the metal rail
of some poor patient's bed,
grinning a welcome,
as the charts go down, and down.

No. Here, you see them sometimes,
in a wisp of spray,
a stretching dog,
an aimless turtle;
hear them in cicadas or goat bells
or the wind.
They glint in quartz,
sparkle on sand,
and relax each time a woman,
middle-aged and lumpy,
makes the brave decision
to be the first one there, that day,
to go topless on the beach.

■ Ledbury is a very special place to me. During the festival in 1999, I first met my future husband there – Pete Brown, another poet (there are two poets called Pete Brown; this was the younger one). Pete ran a troupe called the Gorilla Poets; a mixed bag indeed, including a fruit-tree pruner (Pete), an IT project manager (me), a weapons designer, a radical activist, an ex-RAF man, a born-again Christian charity worker… I think I got in because I had a gorilla suit, which I wore through the town, on a sweltering day, to advertise our activities.

We were quite definitely not part of the Poetry Festival. We stood up and performed poetry to unwitting audiences in pubs, most of whom liked what they heard and asked for more; some even followed us from pub to pub. We were banned only by one establishment.

I met Pete again a few days later at the Festival Poetry Slam, in which we were both competing. In June the following year we were married, and 18 days later Pete died. His wake was held in Ledbury, during the festival, a year to the day after we met. In 2009, my play Once this was a poet, based on our year together, was performed at the festival.

I am aware that other poets have appeared in Ledbury, but to me there has only been one that mattered: Pete Brown. [BR-B]

PETER READING

from **-273.15**

For I will consider our shippe's cat.
For having performed the rolly-polly and curly-paw,
For entertainment she tackles the tenfold cogitations.
For first she frets over rainforest depletions.
For secondly she condems our otiose CO_2 emissions
For these fuck up her atmosphericals.
For thirdly she bids a peremptory adieu to biodiversicals.
For fourthly she regrets that 8 Burmese Pythons,
4 Emus, an Anaconda and 12 Colombian Red-tail Boas
Have been left back at the zoo awaiting *Diluvium*.
For fifthly she grieves the accelerating pace
Of melting Antarctic glaciers
(Smokestack and tailpipe gas)
For these drain the West Antarctic Ice Sheet –
Region containing enough ice
To raise sea levels 20 feet
(Tough luck, Bangladesh, New Orleans).
For sixthly she calculates the numbers
Of *Cuculus canorus* visiting UK
Down 50% in 30 years.
For seventhly she flinches
From the cathode-ray tube's dire tidings.
For eighthly she strenuously denies deities.
For ninthly their accipitrine unleashing scares her shitless.
For tenthly she apprehends devenustation.

Peter Reading (1946-2011) gave his first Ledbury reading on National Poetry
Day in 1997. He published 26 collections of poetry. The festival and WEA
organised an all-day poetry workshop devoted to his work in 2012.

DERYN REES-JONES

from And You, Helen

1

At first, she sees nothing.

Darkness rubs at her – star-blasted, dream-filled – knocking her
                                                    sideways from love,

out of sleep. None of this knows itself. Slow. Forming. Now it is
morning and so there's a shift, when dark is an opening. A heartbeat
on darkness. Pulse. *Pulse*.

This is her mind: connecting with feeling

with thought   with a memory   memory of thought.
Loosestrife. Nettles. She fumbles in spaces, can sense
in the half-light
the breath of her children.

Her body takes root. Her body takes hold.

Roses blacken in a jug at the bedside. Ash in the grate
                                            remembers its fire.

Now it is morning. Yet still there is nothing.

Nothing

but a space beside her.
            Nothing,
            but a space inside.

7

The memory of a memory. That last night returns to her. Fragments
melting in fragments of firelight
His hand that touches, without somehow touching,

                        any human part of her.

It is like this.

—— this slow gorgeous climbing and

gathering,

this entering, this being inside.

White clover, yellow bedstraw, milkwort.

She drops a glass. And now her face, as if something at her heart

had spilled. Or the crack, singing like an ice floe in darkness,

widens   holds.

What she holds,
        she holds for their children. But now there is breakage.
The terrible shifting ocean of herself let out.

Deryn Rees-Jones's *And You, Helen* is a twelve-part meditation (written in collaboration with artist Charlotte Hodes) in memory of Helen Thomas, memoirist, and wife of Edward Thomas. It was commissioned by Ledbury Poetry Festival with funding from the Paul Hamlyn Foundation. The festival's première in July 2014 featured a performance by Juliet Stevenson at St Mary's Church, Kempley, with Charlotte Hodes' collages (animated in a collaboration with multi-media artist Kristina Pulejkova) shown inside the church tower. The illustrated book of the work, *And You, Helen*, was published by Seren, with readings from it included in a BBC Radio 4 documentary of the same name.

CHRISTOPHER REID

'Twixt

There's many a slip
'twixt cup and lip,
and many a knock
'twixt tick and tock,
there's many a trip

'twixt hop and skip,
and many a shock
'twixt axe and block.

There's many a bloop
'twixt spoon and soup,
many a hitch
'twixt needle and stitch,
many a blunder
'twixt lightning and thunder,
and many a glitch
'twixt finger and switch.

There's many a snag
'twixt zig and zag,
and many a hash
'twixt must and dash,
many a botch
and many a hames
'twixt wake and watch
and fun and games.

There's many a trick
and many a trap
'twixt thin and thick
and maze and map,
many a tangle
'twixt line and angle,
many a stumble
'twixt apple and crumble.

There's many a flop
'twixt start and stop,
many a flap
'twixt leap and gap,
many a flip
'twixt down and up –
but many a sip
and many a slurp
'twixt lip and cup,
'twixt bottle and burp.

MAURICE RIORDAN

Feet

We were sitting in the restaurant window
when I heard myself saying *Seamus is here* –
though there was no greeting, And our view was blocked
by a brewery lorry pulled up on the kerb.
I'd no sight of him, but it was nothing spooky either.
What I had seen under the lorry were two feet
passing on the other side. I'd known him by the gait,
as one would by the voice. Yet I'd never before
noticed his feet – and, if asked, I might have guessed
he had a fisherman's walk, slow and deliberate.
But no, what I saw were the feet of a schoolboy
invisibly sandaled, stepping nimbly towards us.

MICHAEL SYMMONS ROBERTS

I Shake Out My Coat

because I cannot sleep and this unsteady
moon has lured me out with promises
to light one final act for me.

Filthy sky-black pea-coat,
I shrug it from my shoulders, grip the collar,
and begin to shake it out.

The stars cannot give second thought
to such a slight shift in the world's array,
yet still they flinch with each down draught.

The backyard breeze, coaxed into mimicry,
awakens fallen leaves from cherries, acers,
laurels, limes, a silvered cloud of tree,

a crack of pylons at the edge of town.
Within an hour, it will be lifting flags
in empty cities you and I have never seen.

I curse myself for waiting days to do this,
given all the places we have been
– turbid rivers, search-lit walls,

dry fields sown with thorns and mines –
no wonder it shakes out so many
splinters, dog-hairs, baggage-tags, such rain.

And given all those half-forgotten places,
it is scant surprise that – *look!* –
my cloth, unfurled, is twice the size.

I had no sense it was so bunched and hemmed,
but now it opens into trench coat, cloak,
black wedding train, tarpaulin, tent,

and still the dross flies from its folds.
I am a vignette: *man-in-silent-yard-sees-light,*
or sings-of-where-he's-been-and-what-he-almost-knows.

O moon, have a heart, my arms are agony,
I cannot stop for fear that when I do,
my old coat will no longer be a fit for me.

ROBIN ROBERTSON

Beside Loch Iffrin
(for Catherine Lockerbie)

Late January, and the oak still green, the year
already wrong. The season miscarried
– the lambs in the field, and the blossom blown –
the whole year broken before it began, and me
standing where winter should have been:
a reived man, a man forspoken.

A woman's kiss will lift you all morning.
A woman's curse will grave you to hell.

By the well-spring on the high moor I saw the day
change colour:
watched lightning root in the far woods;
the sky blink.
Fire-shocks, then a scour of rain, a skail-wind
nagging in through the mirk, scuddering,
dishing it down, rain
turning to sleet, to hail, to snow.
And then
          the cold
– which had been waiting –
          dropped.
The green heath silvered:
every leaf
singled out like rosemary.
The well went milky as a dead eye,
smoked with ice,
though I caught sight of something
as the surface froze –
a clay doll, a *corp criadh*, busied with pins –
and I started down for home.
Where far below I saw the loch-water
going from grey to white: its long fetch

216

shaved by draw-knife, scythe and sickle,
into ice, with the whipped spray turning hard in the air
and splintering on the shore.

The next day, the ice so thick
we cut holes in it so the fish could breathe,
and we gathered round to watch them –
the trout rising – crowding tight
up into a gasp of mouths, silver and pink,
these bright sheaves, alive there in the ice.

Then the cold went down too deep,
and the fish were locked, like till, in the glass.
Birds fell stiff from the sky; every lamb died.
The cows that were left gave more blood than milk.

They found young Neil MacLean, the stammerer,
roped to a tree, libbed, with his tongue
shelled out of his head, dressed in red icicles;
Betty Campbell frozen solid in her bath,
forehead scored with the cross. I saw
Macaulay's mare with the bleed on the brain
going round her field faster and faster till she bolted
straight into the stable wall.
I saw a fox
with a firebrand tied to its tail
going over the high cliff, bundled in flames.
And off to the west, a funeral procession
on the side of a hill where no road lay.

Three months under winter; until winter broke.
They tested the loch with their toes:
the blister of air squeezed
white under the ice, wobbling back
like a spirit levelling.
It took their weight for a while,
till the loch creaked and a mile-long crack appeared
and they couldn't tell what was ice and what was shore:
watching their footprints soften, sink, dissolve,
their hard and perfect world falling to thaw.

A woman's kiss will lift you all morning.
A woman's curse will grave you to hell.

The thing in the well-spring is gone: the clay
worn away to a bed of pins.
I am taken. I am not right; only barely
in the likeness of a man, walking from Loch Iffrin
in a pang of birdsong,
carrying myself
on a hill where no road lies.

MICHAEL ROSEN

People Run

People run away from war:
my father's uncle and his wife
ran away from war.
They ran from one side of France to another.
But the authorities divided people up:
some who ran away were good;
some, like my father's uncle and his wife,
were not so good:
they were not born in France.
So they were put on a list
and had everything taken away from them.
They heard that people like them were
being put on trains and sent away to the east.
So they escaped and ran across France
again.
This was a good move,
they were safe now,
all they had to do was wait.
While they were waiting
the authorities in this place got defeated,
they were seized, put on a train

put in a transit camp, then on another train
to another camp,
where they were killed.
People run away from war.
Sometimes we get away.
Sometimes we don't.
Sometimes we're helped.
Sometimes we aren't.

Because My Parents Were Communists...

Because my parents were Communists
I thought everything they did was Communist.
Not just going to Trafalgar Square
or holding branch meetings in our front room.
Not just shouting at Anthony Eden on the radio
or crying about the Spanish Civil War.
I mean everything.
Like camping, or Marmite.
Camping was definitely Communist
because we went with other Communists.
Marmite was Communist because Mum
said it was good for us.
They liked going into old churches
and my father especially liked old walls.
He loved an old wall.
He knew a poem about an old wall
and sometimes he said it out loud.
Old walls must have been pretty Communist too.
They said they thought the butcher
we went to was very good.
I once heard them recommend him
to some Communist friends of theirs
so he must have been a Communist butcher
I thought
until one day I was playing football
with the butcher's son and he said

that his dad said that we should drop the bomb
on Russia.
Later, much later,
things got much more complicated.
Especially when my mother said,
'I think I'm an anarcho-Stalinist.'

Hwaet!

In 1966
delighted that I had finally turned back from my excursion into Medicine,
I started on a degree in English Literature and Language at Oxford.
I arrived in the English Faculty building to hear a lecture
on *Beowulf*, the first and only piece of epic literature in English.
A woman with a pile of notes in front of her
gave a one-hour lecture on the first word in
the first and only piece of epic literature in English:
'Hwaet!'
That was the first and only lecture I attended
on the course in English Literature and Language.

VALÉRIE ROUZEAU   ■ FRANCE

from Vrouz

When my father shuffled off this mortal coil
Time would not be stomached like that casserole
And dad a feather then my father was so light
Oh how he could have lasted daddy in that state
Of airiness a man becoming angel and so small
My father shrinking with the hope I'd feel
And even though he was as yellow as a clown-fish

In the month of February ninety-seven at the heart
Of just-before-the-spring when he stopped breathing
Ants still ran about and worked without him
Geese would fly without him just the same the moon
The moon would make its circles and its crescents
The big world without a feather daddy would go on.

translated from the French by Susan Wicks

PHILIP RUSH

Dear Andrew

There's authority
in your photo
of the red kite,
its colours sharp
as a bradawl and full
of savoury words
such as chestnut, umber,
ochre and russet.
The winter end
of autumn, last year's
growth a paler shade
of brown amongst
the black-as-Newgate's-
knocker black.
St Lawrence was hazy
when we saw her
with her stilly wing
and forked tail
on border patrol
beside the flood
and the Milebrook.
But a camera cannot

catch the kiteness
of the kite, the muscular
wrench and wrestle
with the wind,
the twist and flex.
An invisible line
binds kite to earth
without which
she could not somersault
and dovetail and pike
in the rainbow air.
This time of year
the hillsides are cloyed
by rainfall,
by the sounds
and significance
of words and syllables
which seep and whisper
into the valley streams.

■ One of the prizes for winning the 2000 Ledbury Poetry Festival Poetry Competition with a poem about percebes and mermaids was a kiss from Carol Ann Duffy; the other was a cheque for £100. The kiss has stayed with me for fifteen years; the cheque left that night, handed over at The Feathers.

It is lovely to see poets in their cages, reading poems from scruffily thumbed copies of books you own and love, and Billy Collins at the Community Centre was a lion of a star and I loved that. But we all know that the real fun of a poetry festival is seeing poets in a more natural habitat. I swear I saw Kapka Kassabova enjoying faggots and chips in The Prince of Wales after her reading and I loved that, too. I was polite enough not to interrupt.

I have a suit which I keep especially for Ledbury and which I wear there every year and hardly ever otherwise; I think it makes me look like an iambic pentameter. I wore my Ledbury Poetry Suit when I read a poem about apples in the orchard at Hellens. My parents said, 'Why are you wearing a suit to go to an orchard?' They had a point. When I got home I pressed the poem under the complete works of William Morris and the juice fermented into a sharp but fruity concoction for which there are no words.

Not all the poetry at poetry festivals is to everyone's taste. I went with a woman I wanted to impress to a reading at Ledbury one year and we sat eagerly at a table towards the front of the hall from which there was no easy exit. The evening did not end well. When I see her now she does not fail to remind me of this. [PR]

The Market House, Ledbury

Like the bottoms
of the great soft
feet of the elephant
the ancient posts
of the market house
shape to what they
meet. Each foot
of the market house
cups to its hump of
anchor stone, none
of them purely flat
or round, so that
each English oak stump
took different work to
ease it down. Like
a patient beast, the
market house has
stood and stood. The
secret of course was
keeping rot away
from the wood.

Kay Ryan wrote and performed this poem at the festival in 2012 ('and a very
pleasurable time I had of it,' she says).

LAWRENCE SAIL

Lundy Headland

I am excited about making sculpture that stands in the wind, the rain and snow, day and night. The sculptures will be like standing stones: markers in space and time, linking with specific places and their histories; catalysts for reflection.

ANTONY GORMLEY

The apparent readings
of mind and eye
at one remove
suggest that the figure
stooping on the headland
is a pilgrim or paying homage
to the wind-flecked ocean

You think to see it
for what it is
until at perhaps
fifty metres
it unmakes itself
to a rusting angular stack
of hollow cubes

When you head back inland
the wind off the sea
follows you as
a voice that utters
he knoweth whereof
we are made he remembereth
that we are but dust

But the voice carries
its own echo
in praise of perception
and the way it can wheel

from one metaphor
of meaning to the next, almost
shaking off the earth entirely

FIONA SAMPSON

Harvest

Already the day
is on the turn as all these days
are on the turn
the light that rose up like
the odour of plums and of vines

beginning its descent
into the earth returning
laden with the voices
of roofers the calls
of blackbirds barks of dogs

hunting beyond the river
who pass between trees
passing to and fro
their shadows are unclear
they do not see themselves

it is we who see them
remembering the dark
as the light turns to the source
again turning once more
to the orange earth.

■ In 1996, I was running what was then the only poetry festival in Wales. It
was an exciting time: the start of my interest in international writing, and of a
life spent advocating the poetry and poets I believe in. I was very young – and

very optimistic! When two fellow-enthusiasts from Ledbury crossed the mountains to pick my brains about how to make a festival work, I was delighted. The more the merrier! And for the next few years, I spent the first week of each July in sheltered housing at Ledbury where, jointly with Graham Hartill, I'd work on a community residency among older people. It seemed that it was always sunny. Even the cottage hospital had a cheerful hum. Enthusiasts invited us into their homes and read us their poems. At the end of the week, we'd have a tea party in the day room of the sheltered housing complex, and everyone would read their work (or we would read it for them). I came to love those long summer evenings when I'd wander the oh so-walkable streets; the tiny tea-room by the festival office; above all – this was before ubiquitous wifi – the escape from daily routine. I always wrote masses at Ledbury. Like its audiences and poets, I got to experience a magical "summer bubble" of poetry. [FS]

JACQUELINE SAPHRA

Everlasting

We never kept spares, and one winter's afternoon,
consigned to darkness again, my mother sent me
across the big road for a sixty-watt bayonet bulb,

ten shilling note in my palm, to the hardware shop
where the lady with the beehive hooked one down
from a shelf of shadows, lifted it from its sleeve

and briefly pondered the condition of the filament
before she eased it into the tester, where it blossomed
and held us blinking in its bright circumference.

Sometimes at night, I lie with all my dead beside me
in the absolute dark, and think of that winter, basking
in the longings of the lost who can't be touched again.

But how to let them go: the hardest task is judging
when it's time to flick the switch and let myself
be blinded by the excess radiance of these times,

226

where, my mother used to say, we had our chance
at the everlasting lightbulb, but in some secret deal,
she claimed, abandoned it.

■ Ever since my first visit to Ledbury in 2008, as first-prize winner (deeply thrilling!), the festival has felt like home to me. From the sofas in the street, to the festive bunting, to the constant flow of delicious food and conversation, every festival brings new joys. But ultimately it is the quality and variety of the poetry and poets that keeps me coming back year after year. [JS]

JANE SATTERSFIELD

Forfeit

> – lost the hawk Nero, which, with the geese, was given away and is doubtless dead, for when I came back from Brussels, I inquired on all hands and could hear nothing of him –
>
> EMILY BRONTË, diary paper, Thursday, 30 July 1845

I know a hawk from a handsaw & when Nero
came crashing down from what wound, what wonder—.

I know a hawk—& the wind running armies
over grasses, hedge and path, the sky unfurled

over a fever of fields, torn petals ferried
on the stream—a hawk, handsome-feathered, rescue-won.

—I know a bite from a beak & when the wanton
spirit rises nothing mournful opens—a day's walk,

the weather fine, sunshine floating free. Bog & bracken,
heather lit from within. I know hilltop, heath & stunted

firs. Thought silt and crow flowers, rue. Thought &
thought again. A proper letter I have never performed.

There must be magic in my taming—cuffs & collars:
the falls are fresh in mind. The hawk's wing-beat's rapid,

can't connive a cage. When clipped, is stripped of dive
& plummet, grip & tear; heart feathered, fettered. Stutter

or hop-to-hand. I thought of rumours, a remembered
sketch, the talon here, the moment tamed. Sift the embers,

scratch the meal; I am seldom troubled with nothing
to do. I have no answers for extreme weather, a failing

source of light. We are at home & likely to be. Or
walking out, I guess, if all goes well, toward the maw

of time. I have no answers but I knew him—hawk quick-witted
as questions in margins, as window-clatter when the clouds

turn cool as iron, ashed in the afternoon. For a while,
a page's torn beauty—I could not countenance a flame.

Line 1 from *Hamlet*. Lines 20 and 22 paraphrase lines from Emily Brontë's
diary papers. This poem won first prize in the 2015 Ledbury Poetry Festival.

MICHAEL SCHMIDT ■ MEXICO / USA / UK

I know the house of course

But who're the seven Gables? *First, papá,*
His portrait in the hall, his portrait in
The library, on the fat chimney breast
In the drawing room, in the pantry too,
Thumbs in his waistcoat, thumbs hooked in his coat,
Thumbs in his trouser pockets; here at last,
The tower bedroom, framed in ebony,
Flabbergasted, fingers in his ears.

*First pap*á, the trail of portraits climbs. He
Down in the garden meanwhile, worsted rump
Busy among vegetables interspersed
With acanthus, rose, with peonies, sweet
Peas, convolvulus, all bleached by summer.
This year's Carrara columns: polished leeks;
This year, Carrara, the white potatoes,
The pale, smudged turnips, bleached asparagus.

In no portrait are his hands as dirty
As they are here, a fist of marl, grim loam,
Manure, gravel, compost, the torn tendrils
Of what the books call weeds (they call them weeds!);
His thumbs, thick as humming birds, are busy
About some business, dig, eviscerate,
Impale. Beside him in Paradise three
Robins triangulate, suing for worms.

Who are the seven Gables? *Meet papá.*
We've met papá. But where's Mrs Gable?
His son? His three fat daughters? Uncle Drew?
You've met papa, the house's metonym.

JO SHAPCOTT

Almandine (Fanny's ring)

A low-burnt coal in an unlit room,
a wolf's eye, a grape from Aquitaine,
a glare, a shadow caught in glass, a shut lid,

night-fog through an alley, a blood-glut,
busted stop-light, a beetle-back, a droop-
dark crocus, a vein-bulge, a bee-mouth,

open, a wine-tanged palate, anger in a stone,
hill-heather, hurt nail, neutron star,
vulval, rosary, winberry, black-red-blue.

OWEN SHEERS

The Dark Seed

I saw your heart today,
a splitting and healing seed
beating in the scan –

a dark pulse suspended
in the white-noise lace
of its downward spreading fan.

A single cell
dividing and joining,
dividing and joining.

A bird's heart, eating time,
and racing you towards us,
out here, watching,

already weighing
your semi-quaver beats
against our own.

I watched your heart
split and heal, split and heal,
and as I did

found myself praying
with a hurting hope
that I might live long

to be your father
but never, please,
to see it stop.

PENELOPE SHUTTLE

The Penelopes

I saw *The Penelopes*
painted and named
but not shamed
on a brick wall
along Calvert Street,
Banksy-esque
I guess,
unsigned urban art,
two young women
on horseback,
en-face.

Though I had my camera
I didn't take a photo,
cameras lie,
they blunt and flatten,
but I kept the white Penelopes
in my eye,
a few days later
it seems
in my mind's eye
they rode on elephants
or camels or elands,
any creature but horses,
and I wonder if I go back
to Shoreditch
(but it won't be tomorrow)
will the Penelopes still be there
drawn by an easy clever hand
low down on a wall
on Calvert Street?

HANNAH SILVA

from The Kathy Doll

The child talks about his mother and as he talks he births her,
his wonderful mother.

As he talks he learns how to breathe,
his wonderful tragic mother.

As he talks he learns how to smile,
his wonderful tragic smiling mother.

As he talks he learns how to laugh,
his wonderful tragic smiling laughing mother.

As he talks he learns how to give,
his wonderful tragic smiling laughing giving mother.

As he talks he learns how to unravel,
his wonderful tragic smiling laughing giving unravelling mother.

As he talks he learns how to fight,
his wonderful tragic smiling laughing giving unravelling fighting
    mother.

As he talks he learns how to lie,
his wonderful tragic smiling laughing giving unravelling fighting
    lying mother.

As he talks he learns how to accuse,
his wonderful tragic smiling laughing giving unravelling fighting
    lying accused mother.

As he talks he learns how to punish,
his wonderful tragic smiling laughing giving unravelling fighting
    lying accused punished mother.

As he talks he learns how to mourn,
his wonderful tragic smiling laughing giving unravelling fighting
    lying accused punished mourned mother.

As he talks he learns how to forgive,
his wonderful tragic smiling laughing giving unravelling fighting
    lying accused punished mourned forgiven mother.

As he talks he learns how to remember,
his wonderful tragic smiling laughing giving unravelling fighting
    lying accused punished mourned forgiven remembered mother.

As he talks he learns how to dream,
his wonderful tragic smiling laughing giving unravelling fighting
    lying accused punished mourned forgiven remembered
    dreaming mother.

KATHRYN SIMMONDS

Launceston
(for Charles Causley)

These are the places you passed by daily,
The same market square and the town hall clock,
These are the hillsides your eye danced over
As you pondered Bayeux or Eden Rock.

The Eagle Hotel and the church of St Mary,
St Thomas, St Stephen, St Cuthbert Mayne;
The castle perched on its round green hilltop,
The cobbled streets warm, or shining with rain.

And mourners still come to visit the graveyard,
And children still read of a dancing bear,
And the great sun turns in the sky as you left it,
And the house you inhabited still stands there.

But the spaces you knew have altered a little,
Cypress trees cleared to let in more light,
These walls display the art you collected,
But others have entered your study to write;

They turn to your life as they open your poems
And find you are gently encouraging still,
Your words go on blazing long after sunset,
Lighting the climb up Ridgegrove Hill.

KEN SMITH

Days on Dog Hill

A season of loose connections, bells
and weddings through the rainy summer.
I woke with my head in a crock,
I had dreamed of nothing.

I'm into town and out, down the hill
and up again, muttering *waggontruss*,
windbrace, through the tall woods
along the old pack road that no longer goes anywhere,

and like the windy leaves never still,
always on the way to some thought
lost in the traffic and the chatter,
the town below fading into voices off,

a hammer's knock travelling beyond itself,
a man shouting his name over and over,
lives made from the sounds they make.
These things do not connect:

a yellow flower from a far off country,
linked hearts cut in a tree's side,
sussura of pigeon wings, an animal threshing
the undergrowth, scribble of bird song

here, here, and your secret names for me –
Old Paint, Wild Root, Scissorbill. I dreamed
the ridge and these massed dark roots of the yews,
anger like a sudden wind. Wild root.

This poem, set in Ledbury, was written when Ken Smith (1938-2003) was the
festival's poet-in-residence, and yielded the title of his 1998 collection, *Wild
Root*.

from **The Caiplie Caves**

[Sauchope Links Caravan Park]

Gulls up at dawn with swords and shields,
if dawn only in low season, in the week

we can afford. My love, who navigated with a Silk Cut
in his wheel hand the unfamiliar roundabout

to the A955 at Kirkcaldy, sweeps droppings
from the paved deck like an owner, with his whole

heart. He grew old not thinking about himself.
So it follows our vacation home is not ours, but let

by the company on certain conditions, for certain uses
pertaining to quiet enjoyment of sea views

beyond the lower lots, signed for
with the understanding our energies likewise

will be applied to the company's benefit.
The dogs we don't have must be leashed, our wireless

fee charged daily. Here is the rent reminding
tenants they don't own, interest confirming

for the borrower to whom the principle belongs.
Here is the insurance to tell us we're not

safe. Here is the loophole which allows it
to not pay. The week he's scraped together is now his.

My old man, who raises his spirit like a lamp,
collects Stella cans tossed from the raceway

down the hill overwritten with gorse and cow parsley;
and who, discovering the bulb beside the door

burnt out, will, cursing happily, replace it with the spare
I laughed at him for stowing in the glove box.

■ I have wonderful memories of the 2015 festival. Inspiring readings. Delightful events. Given the challenges of poetry book distribution, especially internationally, I cherish introductions to new writers, new work, an expanded sense of community, both as a writer and a teacher. Community is so much a part of the Ledbury festival. The warmth and generosity of my host, Anita Scott; the endless food and hospitality and practical answers to impractical questions provided by the volunteers; the conversation. Ledbury is a lovely town. With very good cider. It seems the festival has access to a magical well to the centre of the earth and the centre of the earth is made of cider. [KS]

JEAN SPRACKLAND

lost/lust

Stumbling under the kapok tree,
fevering between its cathedral buttresses,
I am loster than lost in a place
where every known sound has its counterpart:
tap dripping into a metal bucket,
fluorescent tube about to blow,
the flicking of switches, the tuning of radios,
a tent unzipped – the jungle crawls with spies –

and I'm looking for the kind of nest you can find
if you peel back the bark, only it's the nest itself
you're tearing down: a wall, a nursery chamber –
you can't move here without a massacre.

At night I'd know it by the points of bluegreen light,
the larvae glittering in the psychedelic dark,
but by day I need a guide to tell me
this sort good to eat, this one not –

if only I'd been paying attention, not
distracted by the circus of high jinks overhead,
the thought that nothing would induce me –
still it's not for food I want these scurrying things

but for the droplet of liquid inside each one,
because the river-scent I thought I caught this morning
has been atomised by heat
and I know there's a birdcall I should follow to find it again –

but is it the hoatzin, with its smoker's cough,
or the tinamou, wet finger round the rim of a glass?
I've sweated out that wisdom and now I only
shiver and burn to wreck the nest, to put my dry mouth
to the broken place, taste panic and allspice.

RUTH STACEY

Actions Speak

Invitations to bed are soundless;
that moment on the moor shrill wind
shushes and the trees pull their creaks
into their heartwood and watch
the rooks touch beaks on their branches.

Those invites laden with wetness,
caught in a sudden cloud burst
goose skin and clinging gingham,
the second hand copy of Wyatt's
poetry discarded on the picnic blanket.

Suggested with a glance and that subtle
change of expression, the invite
without words: flick of the lace fan,
a handful of flowers (roses of course)
always the rose red and red and bed.

You know the kind of invites I mean?
When the eyes become deeper pools
and you feel the slick pull,
the fascination that drowning holds,
seaweed wrapped around the legs

and the blackness coiled waiting
like a crumpled night sky
that reflects a cavernous sea,
lit only by those strange electric fish
and you say: *you talk too much*

and kiss me to stop the words boil
from my tongue as I try to cling on
to everything; pinning moth winged
letters down in my collection book.
Silently, you show me what is louder.

■ Ledbury Poetry Festival supported my development as a poet by including
me as a participant on their voice coaching course, run by Kristin Linklater. It
was incredible; I went from a nervous performer to a confident one. When I
launched my debut collection at the 2015 festival it was emotional because an
intrinsic part of my poetic journey was the festival's belief in my ability as a
poet. [RS]

ANNE STEVENSON

■ USA / UK

Winter Idyll from My Back Window

(Remembering Jon Silkin's Peaceable Kingdom)

Naked and equal in their winter sleep,
Poplars, ashes, maples, beeches sweep
A bruised agitated sky with skeletons.
Not a leaf. Not a leaf. Lovely generations
Are shrivelling to mulch and mulchiness
Under highway flyovers and underpasses.
A race of acrobatic rats is
Taking place in the bone yard.

Shady rats, showy tails. Is there sex or food
Up there, where bloated pigeons brood,
Silent in wintertime, where Nazi magpies forage
Between raids? Cheeky greys! You manage
Too well, with greed and chutzpah, to keep
Your species lively, running pell-mell to leap
Four times your length, branch to scrawny branch...
! No, you don't crash.

For me, you're jokers in the trees;
For my bird-watching neighbour, enemies,
Though the tits don't seem to mind you
Guzzling from their feeder. The jackdaws, too,
Flap down in a noisy crowd, not noticing.
I don't get any sense that they're competing.
Perhaps these species never think of war,
Not knowing what words are for.

GERDA STEVENSON

Cat-like

(for my father)

'You're like a cat,' my mother told me
when I was young, 'you make yourself better.'
But in that secret, cat-like way,
I've always wondered how that day
would feel when at last it came.
Would I be like a cat *then*?

I used to love cats, but as the day drew near, the less sure
I was about them. I sensed a wild one might be stalking,
as I kept vigil by your bed. I brushed your hollow cheek
with my fingertips, spread your hands over mine,
the silken skin and joints of yours still strangely youthful,
built for stroking liquid melody from ivory and ebony,
the way the Russian maestro taught you. I laced our fingers,
gripped tight, made sure the prowler wouldn't pounce
on my watch: I sang songs, asked for the smile you gave
with sweet grace, an ancient child in that lop-sided curve,
though in your eyes I glimpsed a creature on the far bank
of a slow, dark river, eyeing a gleam of stepping stones.
That day was only yesterday, till then forever in a future time;
it crept in, like cats do, on silent paws, seizing its chance
to snatch you while I left your side to rest.

Now the day has passed, and on a busy street
I glance into a shop window, where a cat yawns
in a patch of sunlight. Our eyes meet. It doesn't know
what happened yesterday, that you've gone.
It blinks, then nestles into itself. I walk on.

in a single breath

questions are hands running fluid, down thighs
around knees, falling into arch, hands brown and
warm and seeking, hands dark and safe, telling
and kissing without need and want of lips and tongues, tongues
lost in palms, palms end in fingertips lost in
napes and dips and buttons of bellies, fingertips
tracing trickling traipsing trying treacherous
against lobe, hairline and cleft of throat, painstakingly slow
yet urgent – throwing away names
stripping
names away, throwing – urgent yet
slow, painstakingly, throat of cleft and hairline, lobe against
treacherous trying traipsing trickling tracing
fingertips, bellies of buttons and dips and napes
in lost fingertips, in end palms, palms in lost
tongues, tongues and lips of want and need without kissing and
telling, safe and dark hands seeking and warm
and brown, hands arch into falling knees, around
thighs, down fluid running hands are questions.

PHOEBE STUCKES

Little Song

I think of tattoos like love, or childbirth;
if it were that painful, everyone would stop it.
We would get by enough on goldfish and biros,
squares of wax paper that sponge on a mark.
I don't believe that everything worthwhile

takes commitment. Takes terror in waiting rooms
and what must amount to foolhardiness.
This girl, first doodled by Picasso on a napkin
maybe, then drawn into my arm with needles
one impulsive Wednesday. She reminds me of you,
how you clutched my hand in the clinic, your nails
digging into my palms, before the nurse came
to take you away. How we both say that it hurt
and anyone who says otherwise is lying.

Phoebe Stuckes was a Foyle Young Poets of the Year Award winner four
years running, from 2010 (when she first read at Ledbury) to 2013, and was
Ledbury Poetry Festival's young poet in residence in 2015.

ARUNDHATHI SUBRAMANIAM ■ INDIA

Tongue

> The tongue is alone and tethered in its mouth
> JOHN BERGER

The man in front of me
is reading
a balance sheet

He is smiling, his gaze
shimmying between columns
effortlessly
bilingual

And though a little drunk
on the liquor of profit

I like to think he is not immune
to the sharp beauty

of integers, simmering
with their own inner life

and I wonder if he feels
the way I do sometimes
   around words

wishing they could lead me
past the shudder
   of tap root
      past the inkiness
         of water
                        to those places

where all tongues meet –

      calculus, Persian, Kokborok, flamenco,

the tongue sparrows know, and accountants,
and those palm trees at the far end
of holiday photographs

   your tongue
   mine

the kiss that knows
from where the first songs sprang

   forested and densely plural

the kiss
that knows
no separation

Five Yellow Roses

What stopped her bawling was the doorbell
ringing, and a man standing there with five
yellow roses, bulked up with green fronds
and tied in a dinky knot with olive twine.

There was no card to say who the flowers
were from. The man's uniform was blue
with a brown insignia of a spider on his right
top pocket that she saw he kept unbuttoned.

As he waltzed down the path to the gate
the Siamese cat that frequented the garden
raised his back and hissed. The man laughed
and flounced out to his waiting white van.

Oh, the shit-faced, side-streets of life! OK,
she'd been born in Madras, in a flowery tea shop
while an albino conjurer magicked a hare
to leap from his heavily ringed brown fingers.

Five yellow roses? Enough to encourage her
to cook saffron rice, with turmeric-tinged prawns
and sautéed yellow courgettes. She didn't play
the Ry Cooder where yellow roses said goodbye.

GEORGE SZIRTES

What she told me about beauty

Hard to lose beauty,
she said, and was beautiful
as she said the words.

It is not the same
later, she said. *Though we say*
it is, it isn't.

And that troubles me
if only for a moment,
she added. *How sad,*

to consider it,
all that gradual vanishing,
all soft power gone.

So she reflected
lost in her beautiful bones,
her beautiful mouth

moving as mouths do
in the saying of such things,
in their full moment.

But that may be what
beauty is, the loss of it
just before the loss,

each moment of it,
she said and took a deep breath
of plentiful air,

the air being good,
the moment just one moment,
that moment, right then.

■ I have had the pleasure of reading and appearing at Ledbury more than once, the last time in 2015 when I was due to do one event but finished up doing three. Ledbury is a beautiful small town and there is a deal of warmth and charm about the festival with everything close. It is one of the three great poetry festivals of the island outside London. It is a privilege to be invited there. [GS]

MACHI TAWARA ■ JAPAN

Two Tanka 2首

1

約束を守らぬ男の笑顔よし
「ばっくれベン」と我らは呼べり

He has a nice smile
The man who doesn't keep his promises
We call him Flaky Ben

2

「大変」が「楽しかった」に変わるとき
旅の終りを知る南風

When 'it's terrible' turns into 'that was fun'
The south wind which signals
The end of our trip

translated from the Japanese by Ottilia Stephens

[These poems relate to Machi Tawara's trip to Ledbury.]

■ My little boy and I enjoyed the atmosphere of Ledbury Poetry Festival. A poet we met at the festival ended up visiting my son Tarō and I back on the island where we live, just off Okinawa. Also, it appears that the student Ottilia

247

who looked after us during our trip has written her university dissertation on the theme of my poetry. I am very thankful for the acquaintances that I made at Ledbury Poetry Festival. [MT/tr.OS]

FRED VOSS   ■ USA

Fist-knock Future

They come back
the old machinists in their pickup trucks bring back their rollaway
    toolboxes
full of wrenches forged before the Vietnam War
retired at age 67 or 68 they come back
at age 70 or 71 rolling their rollaway toolboxes back across the
    concrete floor
the economic crash and their sons
and daughters they thought were gone for good moved back into
    their houses
and their underwater houses and the high prices of medicine forcing
the old machinists back
through the tin door into the shop where they unpack toolboxes
    and cover workbenches
with their measuring instruments they first held when Mickey
    Mantle still gripped a Yankee bat
we talk of all they know about milling machine feeds and speeds
    and the spindle gears of old lathes
how good they are at putting a glass finish on steel with their
    fingers and brains full
of 50 years of machine shop knowledge
then look
at their faces putting on brave 'good to be back' smiles and see
the new lines on their foreheads
the skin sagging
under their jaws the hollow look
in their eyes these men
who thought they had put in the years and fought the war with
    the screaming

of drill bits and foremen
these men who thought they could finally put their feet up for good
and lift grandchildren in their tired arms and laugh back
tying the denim aprons around their waists and stuffing earplugs
    into their ears again
but they will not let us feel sorry for them
as they straighten their backs
stick out their chins like they did when they first picked up a
    micrometer as the Beatles
invaded America and teenagers danced the Watusi and smile
across the sea of workbenches and belt sanders and spinning lathe
    chucks
at the young machinists
so eager to learn
the young machinists
with their hip new beards and tattoos and sides-of-head-shaved
    haircuts
and fist-knocks and dreams
the old machinists
sidling up next to the young machinists to show them a calculator
made the year *Light My Fire* was no. 1
a 12-inch Vernier caliper
made the year Nixon resigned a piece of paper
signed by the astronaut who first stepped on the moon
'Don't give up,'
their smiles say
'Don't give up your chance
to build a better world.'

■ On the evening before my reading with Matthew Sweeney at Ledbury
Poetry Festival in 2008, drinking delicious dark beer at the Talbot Inn and
conversing with my wife the poet Joan Jobe Smith, Bloodaxe Books publisher
Neil Astley and filmmaker Pamela Robertson-Pearce in the alcove, I looked
out the bay window and saw Sir Gawain ride down New Street on his horse
Gryngolet heading toward the gorge and lifting his sword to fight the Green
Knight. I felt the ghost of Hamlet's father down the 450-year-old Talbot Inn
hall and knew Shakespeare must be in the pub downstairs drinking a local
golden brew and mumbling 'To be or not to be' to himself over and over as
Chaucer's pilgrims were stopping along High Street at the Ledbury Market
for apples on the way to Canterbury (they had a mighty long hike ahead of
them). Ledbury will always be England for me. [FV]

MARK WALDRON

Yes I admit that I have ate

that once cool and heavy egg that would
one day have hatched a clever goose of gold.

I cooked it in a pan until it smelted from a hard
into a runny yolk,

and then I promptly drank the molten yellow,
gulped it down and felt it start to burn away

my tongue and gums and teeth whose residue
then blew away as smoke. I felt it coursing down

my roasting throat, through the squiggle
of my blistered viscera,

all the way beyond my screaming shitter
from which it oozed and swarmed and spread

wet metal excrement about my seared balls
and buttocks, before it slowly made to thicken.

And once I'd died of pain, then some time
afterwards I ate away my flesh and bone:

I sank my corpse in acid till no bit of it remained
but just this shiny winding cast, this meandered

single golden sprue that rises from its golden stand,
and displayed like this so well describes a fool.

PHILIP WELLS

Reciting 'Dulce et Decorum est' at the Tower of London

I sang out the pity
To a moatful of poppies
And the faces turned
To a soulful new hope
Where the sad flowers learn
By the stones of our city

How word and her weaving
Still cleaves so close to us;
And the waves of us believing
In a king's voice of peace
Once, are inspired and steering
The fallen and disbelieving

To the seal of a sign
And the sign of a seal:
A sensing at the altar
No altering can repeal;
A footstep with no falter
That dares to cross the line –

The old lie exposed as dross
In the sigh of a silence
Where burned men drown
As we rise to her gentle peace:
The sinking sun of a violin
Over the cacophony of the lost.

HUGO WILLIAMS

African nurses

The little scars on their faces
are the names of their villages,
put there when they were children
in case they got lost.
Their faces are maps
which they carry with them
when they set out across the world
for their new lives.
The scars look like the tracks of tears
cried for their childhood
as they move about their work
in our Northern hospitals.
Is is because Africa is so big
that they have to shout to one another
to make themselves heard?
When they wake me in the night
to give me my medication,
they shout my name
and shine a light in my eyes.
I wake, not knowing where I am.
The nurses and I are homesick
for our lost villages.

MICK WOOD

The Freerunners

Our aim is to take our art to the world and
make people understand what it is to move.

DAVID BELLE

The boys who refuse
to grow up, the spring-heeled
squirrel boys, hands for feet,
feats for brains, nuts

for our estate's great larder
of rotting spaces, have swung
from a ship of winter mist
on ropes of frost and boarded us.

Impervious to cold steel rail
and rimy fence, they reel
around our concrete rigging,
swinging sozzled Gravity

by her crooked arm, bouncing
on the street furniture,
swashbuckling up our stairwells,
steam between their teeth.

From model to sink
we've stuck it out, made paths
that were never on the drawing
board, but to trespass

in that third dimension,
those spaces trafficked by the first
and last lights of the day,
by ocean winds, feels like heresy.

What are we to make
of this hunger for a stale block
and plaza past its sell-by?
Are they mocking us? –

you will never leave this vessel,
your minds are mats,
your hearts are nets,
your hands – is it true? *– are hooks.*

KAREN McCARTHY WOOLF

Up On the Hill

A young Bulgarian
comes to clear the old mattress
and carpet
out of the bedroom

asks if Spring
always arrives so early here?
The forsythia's not out yet
so things must be as they should be.

There's an order
to the colours: snowdrop,
daffodil yellow, forget me not,
brash sunset dahlia.

Up on the Hill
by the edge of Rush Common
where tree-fall debris mingles
with bottle tops, discarded socks

and the crows
poke at the mud – the wrens
are nocturnal now, so
their song might be heard

over the babble of traffic
rumbling up hill like a brook
inexplicably flowing backwards;
they sing, these birds

to the souls
drifting up above the smoke
you can only see from a distance, brown
and insistent as the river,

on nights when we walk,
lips purple with wine, past
the 24-hour shop, arguing about
who said what

and nothing that matters.

C.D. WRIGHT ■ USA

The old business about form & content

I am not among the hardhats dismissive of identifiable content, on
the contrary, but poetry that does not really take language seriously
into account—make that foremost: its texture, smell, shape, strength,
options, registers, tonalities, etymologies, as well as its wide margins
of error; how loudly it can play, how softly, and so forth; poetry
that does not take formal acts into account: those weird, elusive
organising openings that the material presents, whether form is an
extension of content or content is an extension of form, without

obtaining to some sense of form—I cannot distinguish it from prose to any credible degree necessitating it being 'a poem'. Do I contradict myself? Very well then I contradict myself. It's a poem if I say it is. In his notebooks Oppen declared in his declarative way, 'Form is what makes the thing graspable so you can know what is being said and why it was said and how it weighs. Until it takes form you haven't written it.'

C.D. Wright (1949-2016) gave a highly memorable reading at Ledbury in 2013, greatly enjoying her festival visit along with her husband, American poet and translator Forrest Gander, Sophie Robinson (whom she chose to read with her), Gōzō Yoshimasu from Japan and Víctor Núñez Rodríguez from Cuba. She died suddenly in January, from deep vein thrombosis, following a long flight to the US from a festival in Chile.

KIT WRIGHT

Wilhelm

There was a boy who had a withered arm.
It hung there like a permanent reproach,
And he was tortured at the posture farm
And put through horrors by his riding coach.
Infatuated with his English mother,
His need was to supplant her motherland,
Whose hulking navy bullied every other.
He'd cut it down to size with his good hand.

And so it came, when Bismarck got the boot,
Von Tirpitz rose and poured into his ear
The dream of Ocean Dominance. Pursuit
Of this was his one fixative idea...
But when the war-cloud hardened into fate,
He wanted to retract. It was too late.

LUKE WRIGHT

The Back Step

The invoice-chase of Autumn comes
while summer habits linger on
I chain-smoke on the back step
beneath a ten-watt sun.

I know I've got to kick the fags
and get my trainers on again
clear out this yard of summer junk,
and sluice the wheelie bins.

Come Michelmas the rusty walks
will win me round to winsome death
but now I ache for when the wind
had whiskey on her breath!

For fayre and fête and festival
for when the dead of night was light
inebriated clarity
for when the wrongs felt right.

Some days I pass for twenty-five:
I'm ASOS, piss-ups, plans and rage
a scattergun of quips and puns,
and every drink's a stage.

But other days I feel my age
when all my cards have been declined
when sins, like tin cans on a string,
come rattling behind.

SAMANTHA WYNNE-RHYDDERCH

Climbing Helvellyn

Ten years from now the path will look the same,
conceal the same old rocks lying in wait
for the newest ingénues. It's us who will have changed,
morphed from stags to men with mortgages,

yet unsure how, escaping from a feeling
we can't now name and couldn't gauge
the weight of the day we bounded up Helvellyn
camouflaged in tutus and pink antlers,

bantering at the glances of those heading back
to bills shouting from dressers, to sheds
that needed creosoting. Not for us, oh no, we had it all
in the bag: Vodka & Galaxy bars & all the blondes of England

to come. At the summit ten women on a chequered rug
staring at how far they'd travelled, had just begun
to pass round clingfilmed sandwiches as if they were
transparent presents and point little silver flasks

like wands at mountains still to climb
when we fizzed up with hello girls,
having a party? Kind of, they nodded,
we're a support group, we're *Widowed Under 40.*

PETER WYTON

Jack Mapanje Is Gobsmacked

(Ledbury Poetry Festival, 1999)

His audience is homeward bound, well entertained.
He's done his bit. He's back in Hospitality.
A glass of this, a slice of that, and Jack's in clover,
conversational, transparently impressed.
They've closed the streets for poetry! he says,
and he is not far wrong. The Festival's *en fête*,
traffic diverted, barricades in place. A salsa band
has just erupted, Trojan style, from a pantechnicon.
Mood music storms the town. The pubs are full,
hip-swinging crowds congest the thoroughfare.
Big mommas sway. Cool dudes gyrate.
Babies with bulging eyes are held aloft
to view the spectacle. Gangs of small boys
rush to and fro, demented ferrets wriggling
through the adult mass. Sometime next week,
next month, maybe next year, on tour in Africa,
or at some arty-farty Southbank bash,
the mention of a small West Midlands town
will jog Jack's memory. He'll slap his thighs.
His chest will heave. He'll roar, *Ah, Ledbury.*
That's where they close the streets for poetry!

YANG LIAN

from Narrative Poem
(from Part 2, 'Watermint Narrative' (4), Hometown Elegy)

11 *Road*

cicadas declaim in the bent posture of scripture-chanting monks
aesthetics of vast emptiness   a street overflowing with the dawn
three stars planted on my black jade brow
oh cicada song   recite the aesthetics that destroy time
someone who travels in time strips surplus parts away
feeling a cooling weight shift from among the green leaves to
the tamped-down tongue   a lump of jade silently bellows
tiny insect skulls prop up the vault of the sky
oh the vast emptiness is a man setting out shoulder to shoulder
     with the universe
oh the East is letting sweltering blues interpenetrate each other
clavicles locking up every ancient sorrow   above and below ground
I flap silken wings   the beauty of immortality
is solitary in the extreme   on Lakeside Road
I copy father's daily-slower steps
crowded red-brick buildings imitate craggy boulders in the seas
a pincer movement   a raging   cicada visiting its homeland
comes from nowhere and goes nowhere   unless
there's the hardness that's carved along with a tongue
a tongue stretching out from the earth   a demolished distress call
directly   singing a reality that enters deep inside death

12 *Narrative Poem*

there's not a street corner   street name   bus stop
not disclosing us   like language

there's not a weeping willow not drawing the green net tight
to encircle shoals of fish that dart crazily to and fro

let it be called the hometown's   storyline of wandering ghosts
     done wrong
snow calcified in the body banished under a burning sun

black asphalt smoke curing up   the ghosts in the clouds
crave the negatives that will develop the world from its obverse

roast in archaeology a still-unevaporated
instant   of carved columns and painted beams

if you want to summon then summon the flesh tints glutting the
    street
if you want to terminate then terminate   like a mother

hide in a handful of yellow-white ashes
a perfume long ago written down   set on my desk

the thing about narrating body temperature   the thing about
    blood pressure
the thing about a fallen star that shattered above a jet-black
    summit for us

shattered and fallen with the eyes that have no strength to speak
a lump of jade millions of years in monastic asceticism

carefully choose this one and only thing about poetry
wordless structures strip bare numberless dialects of weeping and
    wailing

bypass the starry firmament   slow steps towards father
return to the origin of the allegory of self

Author's note:

In *Narrative Poem*, which is permeated with autobiographical
elements, my father plays an important role. There is a story
about him from his early years: he was born into a wealthy family
whose property included the Fortune Theatre, but, though at first
an enthusiast for Kunqu Opera, he became attached to Western
classical music, and by the time he graduated from university, he
had an exhaustive knowledge of it. His six years as a diplomat in
Switzerland after 1949, served, along with the European way of life,
to convince him even more of the rational beauty which infuses
music. But when the Cultural Revolution began in 1966, Beethoven
was roundly criticised as 'representative of capitalist culture'.

My father faced a painful choice: as a party member he should have trusted the organisation absolutely, yet as an individual, he clearly felt that the music was filled with love and beauty. So which command was he to obey? This problem, now so elementary that it is no longer an issue, was unimaginably grave at that time. If he declared for his own feelings, then how could he not be judged as betraying his family, betraying the road he'd struggled towards for half his life, and betraying the bright future that China had been promised? It was hard, but in the end, he was my father, and finally he chose beauty, though his heart was breaking. He maintained that beauty was not wrong, though the betrayal was. It was only long after I heard this story that I understood: was it because of this that, even while the storm was gathering ominously outside our window, our family was able to preserve a little climate of reason and love, which allowed me to grow up relatively sound and psychologically whole? What I admire is not that he identified with Beethoven, but that this identification itself embodied a kind of strength that emanated from reason, and the strength to re-examine history. So I wrote those lines in *Hometown Elegy* with complete conviction:

bypass the starry firmament   slow steps towards father
return to the origin of the allegory of self

translated from the Chinese by Brian Holton

Narrative Poem is a book-length work by Yang Lian to be published in a dual Chinese-English edition by Bloodaxe Books in 2017.

■ There are hundreds, if not thousands, of poetry festivals worldwide, but to me, Ledbury Poetry Festival is a very special one. I had some great experiences in the two times when I was invited there. Firstly, the town represents a very special depth of the nature and the history of England with all its beautiful and ancient buildings, and thus naturally became the best setting for international poetry. Even more, we were also invited to live with an English family, so the discussions of poetry were not only happening in the events, but at all times days and night, with both poets and Ledbury people, and exchanging poetical understandings with these people brought the poetry down to earth. Thirdly and most importantly, *Concentric Circles*, one of my most important works, was published and launched at Ledbury Poetry Festival when Brian and I were in the festival in 2006. This made an important mark (or a milestone) in the whole journey of my life and writing, because *Concentric Circles* is not only the title of a poem and a book but actually a way of thinking of the global situation and therefore the reaction of poetical mind: we are in One reality in this world, so we are building up One Poetical Tradition crossing languages and cultures now. In 2006, when we were in Ledbury, we felt the centre of our poetical concentric circles was LEDBURY! We do hope these concentric circles will continue to deepen and develop greatly in the future! [YL]

JANE YEH   ■ USA / UK

A Short History of Migration

We boarded a seashell to ride across the waves.
The mythology of our passage involved dirt, sharks, a zeppelin,
    and wires.
We ate the same meal seventeen days in a row (pancakes).
We learned to say yes, please in four different languages.

Our fur-lined hats were useless in the fine September air.
The mystery of our parentage was a serape on our backs.
Out on the prairie, the locals tried to take us at face value.
We learned about sturgeon, washing machines, ennui, and fake tan.

We joined a fruit-of-the-month club to widen our horizons.
The mastery of our foliage required an endless sea of mowing.
We attended bake sales with a suspicious degree of fervour.
We hindered our children with violins, bad haircuts, and diplomas.

Our names were changed to make them easier to remember.
The monastery of our heritage was repurposed into handy snacks.
We sold refrigerators to people who already had refrigerators.
We lived in suburban glory in our newly-built townhouses.

Our children were changed to make them meaner and fatter.
The memory of our verbiage was as a schnitzel in the wind.
We kept our money close, and our feelings closer.
In the event of an emergency, we kept a baseball bat prepared.

In Ledbury, I (*who?*) sang along with the bells, · · · · ·

A muted flap

       of

           love

               deprived (*by whose hand?*)

                 _{mo} _{ga} _{re}   _{té}

              ' 毛・枯・零・【手】'

                            of

                                the wing

By ' *hand/té* = （【手】 손[son]）'

> Who (*I ?*)
>   was sing/ring-ing *be-for(e)* think-ing,......

[

   'R*intrah roars & shakes his fires in the burden'd air;*
   Hungry clouds swag on the deep.'

            R*intrah*   *roars* *(afire)* *in* *the* *ponderous* *air;*
            Cumulonimbus *clouds* *hang* *(hunger)* *over* *the* *deep.*

]

Primordial Ledbury:

            the bottom of the deep

            echoes the church bells graciously

            through its valley, ······

'R*intorah,*······'

The sole of Blake
Rin Tra

          _{Rin Tra}
(鈴, 虎 : bells, tiger)
            = (【Tiger】 범[pɔm], 호랑이[horaŋi])

_{Tiger}
Tra,······

    tí
    té

The soul of Blake
Rin Tra

          _{Rin Tra}
(鈴, 虎 : rin(g), bells, tiger)
            = (【Tiger】 범[pɔm], 호랑이[horaŋi])

    té
    tí

The soul of Blake
Rin Tra

          _{Rin Tra}
(鈴, 虎 : rin(g), bells, tiger)
            = (【Tiger】 범[pɔm], 호랑이[horaŋi])
, · · · · ·
        Lo!-(ro)-ah-
           , · · · · · *z !*

(In Kyoto Goden Miyazawa 29Nov2015 *I saw the master Rikyu's hand:*
The spirit of water, ⋯⋯)

'Finally,'
    = (【Finally】 마침내 [matʃ*imnɛ], 드디어 [tɯdiʌ])
o Ledbury,
the door to another wOrld
    = (【Sliding Shutter】 덧문 [tʌnmun])
                , • • • • •

                     is ab- ou- t t *té* t to Op- en
                                  , • • • • •

   (*'Noreburuda'* = (【Sing】 노래를 부르다 [norɛburɯda])
     'Noreburuda' = (【Sing】 노래를 부르다 [norɛburɯda]))

   (   )

A muted wing-flap
            , • • • • •
                   of
                     love,
                           o,

translated from the Japanese by Sayuri Okamoto

266

■ For Gōzō Yoshimasu, Ledbury is about the church bells; about a little hill behind the house of the (exceptionally hospitable) Bella and Chris Johnson where he strolled ever morning; it's also about a prehistoric memory of being 'at the bottom of the deep' – the place connected to 'water'.

When Gōzō was invited to Ledbury Poetry Festival in 2013 – he was reading his poem 'Namie, or the Blue Door', the poem dedicated to the tsunami and Fukushima victims at the main hall, to be precise – at the precise moment when the bells of the town's monumental St Michael's Church suddenly began to ring and they kept ringing all through the reading. Gōzō felt as if he had been 'called' by 'someone ('who?')', and he, peculiarly and simultaneously, recalled the 'roar' of 'Rintorah' of William Blake's *The Marriage of Heaven and Hell* and the roar of the tsunami waves that had swallowed thousands of people in Japan in 2011; he shifted his talk topic from his Namie poem to the 'spirit' of Blake as if to answer the 'call', as to sing impromptu his song 'along with the church bells'.

Two years later, Gōzō wrote this poem 'In Ledbury I (who?) sang along with the bells' specially for this anthology *Hwaet!*

In this poem, Gōzō tries to answer the poetic spirit of Blake. He experimentally splits 'Rintorah', the word Blake invented, into two (rin & tora) and he adopts two Japanese ideograms (kanji) that respectively sound-out 'rin' and 'tra' and mean 'bells' (or 'ringing bowls' used during Buddhism rituals) and 'tiger'.

He also includes several Korean phonograms (Hangul), some of whose pronunciations remind him of his life-long keywords such as 'song', 'sun', and 'poem'. In doing so, Gōzō tries to see, as he always does in his highly experimental poems, the new chemical reactions taking place between remote languages: between the bell tones and his voice, between Korean and Japanese, and between East Asian languages and English.

To me, Ledbury is all about poetry.

My memory of the place is inseparable from my conversations with the great poets I met there (Forrest Gander, C.D. Wright, Antonella Anedda, Valerio Magrelli, Jamie McKendrick, Víctor Rodríguez Núñez and Kate Hedeen) and with the incredibly welcoming Ledbury people, many of whom are gifted (miraculously) both practically and poetically. I missed the "poetry" or the magic of the place so much that I went back to Ledbury in fall 2013 (and that time, Bella and Chris kindly hosted me at their place again); I wrote my first English poems while I was there.

Gōzō and I hope the town of Ledbury and its Ledbury Poetry Festival will keep attracting poets from over the world, and that we shall come back to our beloved place in near future again. [SO]

BENJAMIN ZEPHANIAH

Things We Say
(song lyric)

Put your ear to the ground
Hear the wholesome earthy sounds of your ancestors
Turning in their humble graves.
Put your ear to the ground
Hear the folk from somewhere before us
Screaming from the belly of the Earth.
Look towards the heavens and ask yourself
Is there a heaven or is that high hell waiting for my sprit to rise?
Raise your fist in defiance
Learn to love your neighbour
As you take the wool from off your eyes.

Put your shoulder to the wheel,
Push forward ever,
Backward never,
Just say no.
Take what you can get for the forces of darkness are working
        against you –
Have a good day.
Put your best foot forward but be careful where you tread
And make sure that your best foot is your friend,
Stand up and be counted,
Lay low and stay alive,
Tell the truth
But if you can't,
Just pretend.

Let's look on the bright side,
Fantasies make brighter days,
But remember that tomorrow never comes.
Go ahead, follow your leader,
As your leader follow leaders,
Watch the wonders of the blind leading the blind?

The blind can be so wise, the wise can be so meek
The meek can be so righteous, strong and bold,
Learn to feel yourself
As you hold yourself together
Like your heroes you are quickly growing old.

Put your ear to the ground and listen to the sound
Of your ancestors singing in the fields,
Do not fear the darkness, hold your head up high
And sing together
More songs forever.
Put your ear to the ground,
Listen to the magic of the music in the dust,
And listen to the words very carefully –
Because you just don't know which words you should trust.

ACKNOWLEDGEMENTS

Many of the poems in this anthology are published here for the first time, and most are previously uncollected. Acknowledgements are due to these sources for previous publication of work included by these poets, in addition to credits included in any notes printed after the poems:

Robert Adamson: *Net Needle* (Bloodaxe Books, 2016). John Agard: *Playing the Ghost of Maimonides* (Bloodaxe Books, 2016). Patience Agbabi: *Ploughshares* (USA). Fadhil al-Azzawi: *Banipal*. Maram al-Massri: *Barefoot Souls*, tr. Theo Dorgan (Arc Publications, 2015). Basem Al-Nabriss: *Granta-Israel* [original publication in Hebrew]. Al-Saddiq Al-Raddi: *My Voice: A Decade of Poems from the Poetry Translation Centre* (Bloodaxe Books/PTC, 2015). Simon Armitage: *Ploughshares* (USA). Shakila Azizzada: www.poetrytranslation.org.

Julia Bird: *Twenty-four Seven Blossom* (Salt Publishing 2013). Alan Brownjohn: *Acumen*.

Ciaran Carson: *The London Review of Books*. Kayo Chingonyi: *The Color of James Brown's Scream* (Akashic Books, 2016). Gillian Clarke: *The Guardian* and *1914 Poetry Remembers*, ed. Carol Ann Duffy (Faber & Faber, 2014). Julia Copus: *New Statesman*.

Mark Doty: *The American Poetry Review*. Carol Ann Duffy: *The Guardian*. Ian Duhig: *The Guardian*. Douglas Dunn: *Archipelago*.

Jonathan Edwards: Ledbury Poetry Festival website. Rhian Edwards: *Scintilla* and *Poetry Wales*. Martín Espada: *North American Review*.

In Athena Farrokhzad's poem 'Ask her' ('Fråge henne'), Swedish idioms or words with no direct equivalent in English have been replaced in the translation with comparable expressions at the author's request. Vicki Feaver: *Poetry Review*. Elaine Feinstein: *Ploughshares* (USA) [earlier version of poem]: 'I have now given it an extra verse and a new title to point up what I intended more clearly.'

Forrest Gander: poem included in a poetry video shown at Ledbury Poetry Festival in 2013 and elsewhere. Azita Ghahreman: *My Voice: A Decade of Poems from the Poetry Translation Centre* (Bloodaxe Books/ PTC, 2015). Vona Groarke: *The Threepenny Review* (USA).

Dominic Hale: *Edinburgh Review*. Tony Harrison: *The London Review of Books*. Robert Hass: *Literary Imagination* (USA). Brenda Hillman: *Poem-a-Day* (Academy of American Poets digital series). Jane Hirshfield: *Brick* (Canada). Matthew Hollis: *The Guardian*. Liu Hongbin: MCLC Resource Center (Ohio State University, 2007). Sarah Howe: poem commissioned by the Magdalene College Festival of Sound in 2015.

Sarah James: *The Rialto*. Jenny Joseph: *Bookmark Poems*, Words Press, Dorchester, 2015.

Kapka Kassabova: catalogue book for *Marti Friedlander: Shadows and Lights*, a solo exhibition of photographs, Auckland, New Zealand, 2009. Jackie Kay: *The Empathetic Store* (Mariscat Press, 2015). Amy Key: *Shabby Doll House*. Mimi Khalvati: *Jubilee Lines: 60 Poets for 60 Years*, ed. Carol Ann Duffy (Faber & Faber, 2012).

Nick Laird: *The Poetry Review*. Valerie Laws: *Ofi Press magazine* (Mexico). Gwyneth Lewis: *The Spectator*. Liz Lochhhead: *The Guardian*. Michael Longley: *Sea Asters* (Fine Press Poetry, 2015) and *The New Yorker*. Hannah Lowe: *The Yellow Nib*.

Roger McGough: *New Statesman* [earlier version of poem]. Jamie McKendrick: *The London Review of Books*. Nikola Madzirov: *Modern Poetry in Translation*. Bill Manhire: *The London Review of Books*. Jack Mapanje: *POEM*. Kei Miller: poem commissioned in 2015 by the Poetry Society as a response to the exhibition *Gold* at The Queen's Gallery, Buckingham Palace. Adrian Mitchell: *Come on Everybody: Poems 1953-2008* (Bloodaxe Books, 2012). Reza Mohammadi: *My Voice: A Decade of Poems from the Poetry Translation Centre* (Bloodaxe Books/ PTC, 2015). Kim Moore: York Mix Poetry Competition website. Helen Mort: *The Compass*. Togara Muzanenhamo: *The White Review*.

Katrina Naomi: *The Poetry Review*. Tal Nitzán: *At the End of Sleep* (Restless Books, New York, 2014).

Sean O'Brien: *The New Yorker*.

Ruth Padel: *Interlitq*. Brian Patten: 'The Minister for Exams' © Brian Patten 1996, by permission of the author c/o Rogers, Coleridge & White Literary Agency. Pascale Petit: *Ploughshares* (USA). Clare Pollard: *The Dark Horse*. Craig Raine: *The New Yorker*.

Mohan Rana: www.poetrytranslation.org. Peter Reading: *-273.15* (Bloodaxe Books, 2005). Deryn Rees-Jones: *And You, Helen* (Seren, 2014). Maurice Riordan: *Ploughshares* (USA). Michael Symmons Roberts: *Poetry London*. Robin Robertson: *The London Review of Books*. Valérie Rouzeau: *Talking Vrouz*, tr. Susan Wicks (Arc Publications, 2013).

Fiona Sampson: *The Catch* (Chatto & Windus, 2016). Jacqueline Saphra: *The Rialto*. Ken Smith: *Shed: Poems 1980-2001* (Bloodaxe Books, 2002). Jean Sprackland: *The London Review of Books*. Ruth Stacey: *Envoi*. Anne Stevenson: *Stand*. Matthew Sweeney: *Poetry* (USA).

Mark Waldron: *Meanwhile, Trees* (Bloodaxe Books, 2016). C.D. Wright: *The Poet, the Lion, Talking Pictures, El Farolito, a Wedding in St Roch, the Big Box Store, the Warp in the Mirror, Spring, Midnights,*

Fire & All (Copper Canyon Press, USA, 2016). Samantha Wynne-Rhydderch: *The Compass*. Jane Yeh: *The New Republic* (USA) [earlier version of poem].

Benjamin Zephaniah: revised lyrics (previously unpublished) to song from *Naked* (One Little Indian, 2010).

Special thanks are due to the Poetry Translation Centre for permission to include five translations of poems by poets who have taken part in three events at Ledbury Poetry Festival over the years: Al-Saddiq Al-Raddi, Shakila Azizzada, Azita Ghahreman, Reza Mohammadi and Mohan Rana.